Alison

Cheers!

Shy

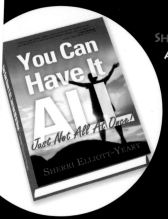

Praise for *You Can Have It All, Just Not All At Once!*

Treat yourself, early in the morning with your coffee, sitting in a comfortable chair on the deck, or late in the evening when the day is done, to Sherri Elliott-Yeary's new book, *You Can Have It All, Just Not All At Once!,* and you'll be refreshed, relaxed, and reenergized. It's never too late to motivate. In sharing the stories of the special people covered in this book you will discover a whole new lease on life.

—Ebby Halliday
Founder, Ebby Halliday, REALTORS

The stories Sherri shares in her new book, *You Can Have It All, Just Not All At Once!,* helped me get one step closer to empathy—empathy for the daily and life challenges that women face, which are well-masked from men. I once was the operating partner in three child development centers with over sixty-five female employees. Although I tried to understand and empathize with their struggles outside of work, I think I just scratched the surface. As I read through these personal stories, I think about how many courageous women I have worked with every day just trying to find happiness and balance in their lives. Their chins were up and that's all I saw as a man. For those women I thought I knew, I'm glad Sherri's book was written, and I hope all women find their balance and joy in life through these pages.

—Clint Haggard
Fifth Generation, Haggard Family Advisors

Sherri's new book, *You Can Have It All, Just Not All At Once!,* is a thought-provoking departure from the typical approach to "having it all." It takes the reader through real-life challenges that courageous women have met and managed, and through which each has found new strength, renewed hope, greater determination, and the wisdom to know what really matters in life. Sherri Elliott-Yeary brings a refreshing new approach to having it all: one that is within the reach of virtually everyone. Beautiful!

—Dr. Sherry Buffington
CEO, Author and International Speaker

You Can Have It All, Just Not All At Once! is a refreshing balance that blends the struggles with the strengths of living a full and potent life. Understanding that desire alone does not make one move from struggle to freedom, the women who so courageously share their struggles also inspire with the ways they move on with power and grace. Sherri Elliott-Yeary provides practical information and tools that women can implement immediately, but, more importantly, these stories provide hope that even in the ordinariness of life one can be fulfilled. Just as she did for women with addictions, Sherri helps other women incorporate the HOW (honesty, openness, and willingness) essentials for recovery from anything.

You Can Have It All, Just Not All At Once! touches your heart and fires up your mind to "accept life on life's terms" and flourish in doing so. Here are stories of exceptional women who have the courage to somehow let us see the struggle, the inside story, and how to still live a full "outside" life. Sherri Elliott-Yeary provides hope to women with various life concerns. Watch out: you may find hope that things can be different and the "courage to change the things you can."

—Brenda J. Iliff
Clinical Director, Caron Texas Treatment Centers

You Can Have It All, Just Not All At Once! is a book about real women and the inward and outward challenges women struggle through each day just living life. Marriage, career, motherhood . . . life can be hard, but there is always hope. Sherri captures the soul of women. As I read Sherri's book, I felt like I was at my kitchen table having coffee and sharing stories with intimate friends. It is a book women will love and use as a source of encouragement and hope.

—Jodie Laubenberg
Texas State Legislator

I enjoyed Sherri's new book, *You Can Have It All, Just Not All At Once!* I think women of all ages and stages of life will enjoy this refreshing read; there is insight for everyone in this book. You will glean a healthy bit of knowledge from the vignettes presented!

—Kimberly McMillin, MD
Specialist in Family Practice, Baylor Healthcare System

Sherri has once again combined her intelligent and heartfelt insights with her personal experiences, as well as the experiences of others, to challenge us to live our lives to the optimum. This is not a book to read once and set aside, but rather to spend time with, revisit, and draw a new and fresh lesson based on where your journey has taken you since you last picked it up. This is a book to share with those dear to you.

—Nancy Ackley-Ruth
Cultural Expert, Africa and Middle East Specialist

A thoroughly inspiring book of real women facing seemingly insurmountable struggles and how they have survived and triumphed to achieve victory. Full of great advice for all of us who will face extraordinary challenges in our personal and professional lives and can benefit from the stories and advice in this thoughtful, emotional, and enlightening book.

—Valerie Freeman
CEO, Imprimis Group, Inc.

True success is living the life *you* want to live, to be content in your own skin, and to have the courage to overcome emotions like guilt and fear to realize your dreams. Sherry Elliott-Yeary is a woman who has achieved a wonderful balance of personal and professional success. Her latest book features women like her, who will inspire you to go for it! As my granddaughter says, "Girls rule!"

—Shivaun M. Palmer
Founder, Executive Producer and Host
Women's Broadcast Network, LLC

Sherri's book was a gentle but firm reminder to take stock right now of what we have in our lives and to appreciate our blessings. Her stories are insightful. Sherri's advice is practical yet inspirational. There is a message for everyone.

—Jill Malouf, Esq.
Dealey, Zimmermann, Clark, Malouf & Gray, P.C.

Perhaps the most astonishing aspect of this book is the realness with which the stories are conveyed. There is a lesson for all of us: living a full life not only takes tremendous courage, but also requires support from others who care. I think the best message for women is for us to stop trying to do it all by ourselves and to let others help and inspire us. This book is a great start!

—Dr. Alise Cortez
Professional/Organizational Development Consultant

You Can Have It
ALL

Just Not All At Once!

SHERRI ELLIOTT-YEARY

Brown Books Publishing Group
Dallas, Texas

You Can Have It All, Just Not All At Once!

Brown Books Publishing Group
16250 Knoll Trail Drive, Suite 205
Dallas, Texas 75248
www.BrownBooks.com
(972) 381-0009

A New Era in Publishing™

Hardcover ISBN 978-1-61254-048-1
Paperback ISBN 978-1-61254-083-2
Library of Congress Control Number 2012935974

Printing in the United States
10 9 8 7 6 5 4 3 2 1

For more information or to contact the author, please go to:
www.GenerationalGuru.com or www.RealWomenHavingItAll.com

This book is dedicated to the women who are purposefully choosing to live an authentic and powerful life while trying to have it all. We only have one life to live—make it count!

We tend to forget that happiness doesn't come as a result of getting something we don't have, but rather of recognizing and appreciating what we do have.

—*Fredrick Koenig*

Contents

Foreword by Karla K. Morton
2010 Texas Poet Laureate

Upon reading the initial chapters of *You Can Have It All, Just Not All At Once!*, I kept feeling everyone had gone through a similar kind of darkness, and I wanted my poem to convey a feeling of hope that says, "Yes, we can hold that great golden ball (our greatest wishes) in our hands," though perhaps in a way we hadn't thought of before, a way we had to learn about, a way that's safe for us . . .

Eclipse
So many ask about that time,
that fear.
There is no doubt I remember
the darkness – long somber nights
zipped coffin tight around my body.
And in those months –
those deep, heavy months –
I learned to stop struggling
to find answers
in the world around me
and closed my eyes,
and felt a golden pinprick of light
welling up inside –

smaller than those holes we punched
in papers
in the fifth grade
during solar eclipses;
never once doubting a teacher
who made magic from Science and God;
who taught us to witness
that unseen beast of Sun
in full form, on the sidewalk;
holding its greatness in our hands;
believing this is what mere humans
are only meant to see.

Acknowledgments

A book like this is not the effort of any one person. There have been many people along the way who have helped and supported me in my work. I'd like to thank some of them specifically.

I wouldn't have been able to survive both the writing and marketing process of this book if it were not for the unwavering encouragement and enthusiasm of my husband, Dr. Mason Yeary. His ability to lovingly provide feedback on each chapter day or night made writing this book possible. His honesty, even when I didn't want to hear it, helped me grow both as a person and as a professional. Equally crucial is his complete faith in my work, along with a large dose of patience and understanding. No words can describe how much his support has meant to me throughout this process; without him there this book would not have been possible.

To my mom, for giving me life and helping me understand where I came from; this insight has given me the strength and courage to discover my true gifts and talents.

To Denise Vadala for showing me what unconditional friendship truly means. I miss you every day.

Thank you to my daughter, Khirsten, for accepting and loving me as your mom, even when I am "getting in your business."

Thank you to Jessica and Meredith for allowing me to play a role in your lives as your dad's wife.

I am grateful to have the opportunity to thank others who have made this work possible. It is more for the benefit and cleansing of my soul as the writer to admit the help I have received from others, than it is for them to read it. For without a doubt, this book would not exist had it not been for the help and influence of those individuals in my life who have patiently endured my arduous journey from brokenness to wholeness.

Included are interviews and comments from some of the most powerful women I know—women who are just like you and me, who want the same things: a great career, a loving family, time to enjoy life and personal interests, and a close bond with God—or with whoever He is to you.

Am I the right messenger to help other women? I believe that many of us are, and whenever I doubt myself, I know that's my inner critic trying to take me off the course God has chosen for me.

Many thanks to the women who have graciously shared their stories with me; it is always a risk to confide in an author. You never know where you'll read about your most guarded secrets. But thank you for trusting me by revealing your hearts. Your stories are sometimes painful, sometimes hilarious, but always honest and helpful. Thank you for being willing to be broken and fed to the masses. God bless you for your courage.

My heartfelt gratitude goes to the women of my Passionate Organization of Women (POW) Group—Veronica Thomison-Perez, JoAnna Couch, Jennifer Null, Alise Cortez, and Kimberly Davis—for listening to me and being present when I needed you most. Ladies, you are not only terrific mentors, you are awesome friends.

Special thanks to Petey Parker, the champion of Consult P^3, and the women on our faculty who stepped up and shared their stories and networks to make this book happen. I am forever grateful to this group of dynamic women, including Dr. Eileen Dowse, Jan West Tardy, Maura Schreier-Fleming, Mary Golaboff, and Blanche Evans.

To Karla Morton, 2010 Texas Poet Laureate, the first female in almost twenty years to receive this honor and distinction. Thank you for contributing an original poem to the book to share with our readers.

Thank you to Milli Brown and to Brown Books Publishing Group for getting this book into the hands of the readers.

My deepest appreciation goes to you, the reader. Whether you're a corporate executive working sixty hours a week, a single parent trying to raise a family, or someone who's tired of feeling stressed out and pressed for time, this book is for you. May it bring you answers, guidance, comfort, and support as you try to "have it all."

Sit back, relax, and enjoy the experiences of others who have been there, done that, and even got the T-shirt. They want to share with you what they have learned.

As one humorist put it: "You must learn from the mistakes of others, you can't possibly live long enough to make them all yourself."

Introduction

For as long as I can remember, ever since I was a small child, I have been mesmerized by butterflies. I love how they appear to float effortlessly and look so delicate and beautiful. As a butterfly emerges from its cocoon, it struggles and strains to free itself. This struggle is essential to strengthen its wings and shrink its body. Otherwise, the butterfly's wings would be weak, its distended body ungainly, and it would never be able to fly gracefully.

Sherri at age seven

Butterflies everywhere that endure this struggle are rewarded with the glorious adventure of exploration, flying from blossom to blossom.

The women in this book share their most intimate stories of successes and setbacks on the road to building and living life to the fullest. All of these extraordinary women and I have one thing in common: We believe that having it all isn't about competing with others. It's about powerfully choosing the life you want—the life that works for you as a woman—so you can live your life to the fullest and fly gracefully from blossom to blossom.

As women, we are constantly emerging from our cocoons, struggling and straining to become free, strong, and beautiful. Growth of any kind cannot occur without enduring some pain and discomfort. And with the lesson of the butterfly, we must acknowledge that cocoons don't fly.

We women often try to fly while carrying baggage we don't need on our backs, beating our wings until we're exhausted, never realizing there is a better way to live life.

My personal perception of "having it all" is a momentary state of mind. It's an appreciation for those moments in life when you recognize the blessings you have been given, before the next curve in the road appears. If we look beneath the obvious and see that "having it all" is more a state of mind than a state of existence, then we are able to clearly appreciate the life we have chosen in all of its beauty.

The inspiration for this book was born from a deep, personal place in my soul. My passion is to help women like me transform the life they are living today. We can live an authentic and powerful life by clarifying who we are and what we want, and finding a path that leads us from aspirations to reality.

This book shares stories of how women emerged from the cocoon of unintentional living to embrace a powerful, intentional life filled with grace, gratitude, and love.

What would your life look like if every moment of it were absolutely enriched, fulfilled, and swelling with joy? A life where your health, relationships, career, spirituality, and finances are the best they can be? One in which you greet each day with energy and enthusiasm for whatever comes your way? What would you give to accomplish that?

Not too long after I authored my first book, *Ties to Tattoos*, I was having coffee with a friend who is a wellness counselor. I was complaining about my need to rebalance my life due to new business and speaking requests.

He looked at me and said, "Make a list of all your blessings, and when you're done, ask yourself, 'Which one would I give up to take away the stress?'"

I was stunned and said, "None!" Not my health, business, friends, family, new book, anything. I was grateful for all of these gifts, and then I suddenly realized the point he was trying to make: We can't have it all without life's challenges to make us grateful for the blessings we have, at each and every stage of our lives. We have to "pull up our big girl pants" and accept all that comes with life, including the tough stuff.

With the gifts and talents God has blessed me with, I understood at that moment that it was my responsibility to use them and quit complaining. I've had my share of "Why me?" moments, but I tried my best, learned from my mistakes (at least the ones I'm aware of), and moved forward in a new direction to achieve my goals.

It's been very liberating. Through ups and downs, I've built a successful, challenging, continuously evolving consulting business that I love, replete with a wide network of relationships that reward me with joy.

I rise every day excited about the opportunities ahead and ask for the emotional, physical, and mental energy to accomplish everything on my busy schedule. I would not be here today if I hadn't made and kept these essential promises of living a balanced life to my family and myself.

We all know we feel amazingly energetic when we discover something we are passionate about. I mentioned to my husband that this would be the last book I wrote, and he looked at me and said, "Sure, but you won't be content unless you have a new project to start after this one."

He's right, of course. When I get interested in a new project—whether it is helping a friend find a new job, or learning a new skill—I take it on 150 percent with my hair on fire.

That's what "having it all" means to me: taking the good with the bad and doing the best you can with what you've got.

What does having it all mean to you? To find out, I contacted dozens of women and asked them to share their stories, insights, and advice. Not everyone participated but, to my humble amazement and deep appreciation, most did.

The contributors in this book are friends, business contacts, and women who were recommended to me. They each have unique, yet familiar, stories to tell about jobs, ambition, marriage, family, finances, time spent with God, and trying to fit it all in the same twenty-four hours we each are given every day.

These are the women anyone would look at and think, "She has it all." What you don't see is that these courageous women have each overcome something that could cripple or destroy the strongest among us. Instead, these women emerged victorious. They learned the powerful lesson that having it all means making tough choices that put their lives back in balance.

If only one story touches your heart and fires up your mind then I've fulfilled the mission I set out to accomplish. My personal motto that may help you as you embark on this journey is "Never give up, never surrender."

So curl up in your favorite reading chair, let the phone go to voice mail, and enjoy!

If you can dream it, you can achieve it!

Sherri

1

If You Really Have It All,
You Probably Want
to Give Some Back!

"Life's challenges are not supposed to paralyze you;
they're supposed to help you discover who you are."
—Bernice Johnson Reagon

*What does the phrase "having it all" mean to you? For most it means being
well-rounded: you have a good education, a satisfying job, a loving family and
circle of friends, a healthy spiritual life, fun hobbies, and time to give back
to the community. But if you're like most women, having it all also means
you're overscheduled, terrified of failure, exhausted, and running on empty.
Is that what you really want? If not, it's time to evaluate where you are and
where you want to be.*

Sherri Elliott-Yeary

Every choice we make leads us in one of two directions. We are
headed either toward a future that inspires us or toward a past

that limits us. When we're moving in the direction of our deepest desires, we feel the support of the entire universe behind us, and we are inspired by our lives. Our excitement wakes us up each morning and gives us the motivation and energy we need to forge ahead.

It doesn't matter what our vision is, whether it's to make a million dollars, to spread love to the neighborhood kids, to introduce a new law into action, or to become a teacher in middle school. When our actions come straight out of our vision for our lives, we radiate joy and passion that effortlessly carry us through the days.

Making choices that support our dreams gives us a tremendous sense of empowerment and self-esteem. When we see we are making progress toward what we want out of our lives, we feel powerful, hopeful, and confident. Making choices that move us forward gives us the confidence to manifest our goals and desires.

On the other hand, choices made from fear keep us tied to the past. Our need for safety, security, and predictability prevents us from stepping outside the reality we know. Afraid of what we might find outside the comfort zone of what is familiar, we stay tied to the past, even when it no longer fulfills us.

Our outer world reflects our inner commitments. If we want to know what we're really committed to, all we have to do is look at our lives. We are, whether aware of it or not, always creating exactly what we are most committed to. It is vital to understand that the choices we make are always in alignment with our deepest commitments. By examining what we have and what we don't have, we will be able to uncover and see what we are truly committed to. When our lives are not the way we want them to be, we can be certain that we have a conflicting, hidden commitment to something other than that to which we say we are committed.

Since most of us were never taught about underlying commitments, we are unaware that they even exist. But uncover them we must, because as long as they remain hidden, our underlying commitments will continue to dictate our choices. We will be left to experience the stress and struggles that go along with saying we want one thing while doing another. We will continue to feel the powerlessness of not being able to attain the future we desire.

Do you long for a new life filled with joy? More time for yourself? Would you like to take better care of your health, reduce stress, and create more balance in your life?

You're in good company. Many of my female clients and girlfriends have often shared that they spend so much time on the phone or computer communicating with people for business that they no longer have the energy or desire to talk with their families or friends when they get home. As a result, their soul-nourishing relationships start to deteriorate and they end up feeling empty.

As women, we often try to fill the holes inside of us with overspending, overeating, or overmedicating as we continue to drive ourselves to an ever-higher level of success and become disappointed as the emptiness remains. Could it be that our lives, our purpose for being here, are not connected to our job titles, where we live, or the size of our portfolios?

Many of us, myself included, get too caught up in stuff we think is important and fail to protect and nurture what is most important to us so we can lead fulfilling lives: our relationships, our passions, and our souls.

Like most of my friends and colleagues, I was so busy trying to survive my life I had no soul left to live it. I was trying to have it all, all at once, and I was paying the price.

If you desire a life that is fulfilling, you have to let go of toxic

3

relationships, guilt, and other burdens. Only then will you have the opportunity to experience a life of joy.

In other words, you can have it all, but don't expect or demand of yourself that you do everything all at once. Working until you collapse into bed at night is no way to live, and it's no way to treat your family either. Yet, as women, we continue to push ourselves, day after day.

Taking the risk to follow our hearts gives us energy for our future and breathes life into our dreams. By stopping and asking ourselves if what we are doing is leading us toward an inspiring future or away from it, we gain the opportunity to remember our visions for our life. Then we can honestly see how many of our choices are leading us in the right direction and how many are leading us astray.

This question can alter your life in an instant because as soon as you realize you're headed in the wrong direction, you have the power to make a new choice, a choice that can deliver you the life you desire.

I personally have to remind myself to stop struggling long enough to smell the roses. As a reminder, I carry a piece of paper in my wallet that states, *"Haste will take the place of peace and grace if you are not proactively choosing how to live your life every day."*

By clearing a space in my life to be still and listen, I can hear the messages of serenity, hope, and love more clearly. Only I can keep things in balance to achieve the life I want, which is to inspire and serve as a role model for those lives I want to touch.

My daughter, Khirsten

When you're present in life, you pay attention and see and hear small things in the world. If I had been listening more closely, I might have been more help to my daughter sooner.

Khirsten is my only child. When she was in her first year of college, she moved away from home. I missed her, but I knew this was a journey both of us had to experience.

Within six months of being away at school, Khirsten had lost a lot of weight—probably forty pounds—and had developed very bad acne. I was clueless, and only asked her if she was eating the right foods. Her response was that she had been studying a lot and did not remember to eat and that was why she had lost so much weight. I believed her. She gave me the answer she knew I wanted to hear: that everything was OK.

A few months later, I received a call from Khirsten's college apartment manager advising me that Khirsten's apartment was under surveillance by the Drug Enforcement Agency. I was shocked and terrified at the same time.

I later discovered Khirsten had been using methamphetamines (meth) for almost a year. She was introduced to drugs by a fellow student who told Khirsten that meth would give her extra energy to study and help her lose weight.

When I talked to Khirsten about her addiction, she would not share anything with me. In fact, she threw me out of

5

her apartment—the one I was paying for while she skipped class. I eventually took her car away so she could not use it to hurt anyone, as she was allowing her live-in boyfriend, a.k.a. the drug dealer, to use the car to sell drugs.

I was petrified, unable to sleep or eat with the fear my phone would ring with news that Khirsten had been arrested, or worse . . . that she had overdosed or was dead.

Shortly after, during a trip to San Antonio with Khirsten and my brother Terry, who was visiting from Canada where my family still lived, Terry and I couldn't help but notice how thin Khirsten had become and the intensity of her need for a fix, which resulted in uncontrollable fits of rage at times.

Terry and I were both concerned that she was so far gone that neither of us could reach her. When we dropped her off at her apartment, we noticed her apartment door had been smashed in and her place was destroyed. A drug dealer had broken in and stolen everything she owned, including the car she had just gotten back from me. (Don't say it . . . I already know.) This man even took her pit bull, Mia.

At that moment, I hit my bottom—never mind her bottom—and informed her that if she did not go willingly to treatment (because legally she was an adult even though she was not acting like it), I was no longer going to pay to support her while watching her destroy herself.

Khirsten agreed to treatment with one condition: we had to find Mia. I agreed because, at the time, Mia was the only thing

6

Khirsten seemed to care about. The drug dealer ditched the car on the other side of Dallas with Mia still in it! Mia was able to chew her way through the seats and escape from the car; somehow she made her way back home. I know God had a hand in this.

You can't imagine the amount of paperwork and insurance requirements to transport Mia, a "dangerous breed," across the border to Canada on an airplane, but we did it. It's amazing the strength one can muster when the moment calls for it!

The day I left my only child, a twenty-year-old, in a treatment center in Calgary, Alberta, Canada, I told her how much I loved her, but I also made it perfectly clear that if she walked out, she was on her own.

I looked back at her as I walked to my car. I felt like I had just lost my baby and clutched my stomach from the pain of the loss and my fear for her life. There was nothing more I could do to help her; it was time for her to stand up and choose her future.

I was barely able to keep my new consulting business afloat while trying to survive Khirsten's addiction. I understood there were things I could change and things I couldn't, but the quality of my life would always depend on the quality of my inner life, not my outer life. I did a lot of praying during this difficult period.

I am proud to share with you that Khirsten has been clean for more than four years and is living life on her terms. For that, I am deeply grateful. We cherish every minute we have together and do not take anything for granted.

I am often asked what I would do differently and I answer that I would not change a thing. I could blame myself, blame her, blame others, but that's a burden I choose not to shoulder. Instead, out of our journey from her addiction, I learned the value of life and to appreciate and cherish the everyday moments.

During the flights back and forth to Canada to check on Khirsten, I embraced the silent periods of time and, during those moments of reflection, I started thinking about my daughter from a generational perspective and began to wonder what others of her generation were facing.

This was life-changing for me, and it was the genesis of a new passion: to understand and to share with others the hurdles our next generation of leaders are facing and how we can support them to be successful in life. That's when I wrote my first book, *Ties to Tattoos: Turning Generational Differences into a Competitive Advantage,* and dedicated it to Khirsten. She inspired me with her courage and determination to turn her life around.

The message below is from Khirsten after I shared with her that I had dedicated *Ties to Tattoos* to her:

It means so much to me that it is hard to explain. First, my mom not only found me help at the best possible treatment center, but it was far away from her. My mom knew I needed to leave Dallas to help me overcome my addiction to meth and stay clean by removing me from my sources. Mom knew that being close to my family in Canada would give me the physical support she may not have been able to give me all the time from three thousand miles away in Dallas. Mom knew in her heart that even though it would be hard to leave me so far away, it was the best thing for me and that my family in Canada would be available to help me whenever I needed them. My mom had to learn to let go and believe in me. I can't imagine how hard that was on her, but she stood by me every step of the way during my treatment and gave me the strength to carry on so I could actually work on my issues on my own.

During my treatment I remember my mom mentioning a book she was writing, but I never really paid much attention at that time as I was dealing with my own struggles. When I was in treatment, she told me more about the book and what it was about on one of our many daily long-distance phone calls.

As she was already so busy with new business, I really didn't fully understand why she was taking the time to write a book until much later when she shared with me that her writing was an opportunity to focus on something other than our struggles, and it gave her a sense of peace. I am so happy my mom found her own healthy outlet to express her feelings while I was going through treatment in a positive way instead of stressing on the inside and carrying it around all bottled up like a ticking time bomb. I am so unbelievably proud of her, for how hard she has worked on her book and the difference her book has made to other members of my generation—the millennials. When mom told me she dedicated her first book to me, I was so touched I cried. I never thought anything good would come out of my addiction, but now I know that something has.

My mother is my hero because she held me up and gave me the strength to overcome my addiction when I never thought I could do it. I have been clean for four years now because of this woman; if I had not had my mom there loving and supporting me during some of my darkest moments—when I didn't think I could possibly go on any longer—there is no way I would have made it through. My mom is everything to me: she is my mother, my savior, and my best friend, as well as my hero. I would not be alive today without her.

When I would call her crying, telling her to get me out because I could not do it any longer—because my meetings had been horrible that day and had brought back up so many terrible feelings—she would talk to me, listen to what my thoughts and feelings were, then calm me down and act as my rock of support.

At the worst point in my addiction, I knew I wanted to get clean and no longer live that kind of life, but I lacked the strength to do something to fix it. My mother was there to save me. She gave me the out I had so desperately needed for so very long, and I grabbed on to it and held tight—and look at where I am today. There is no way I would be alive today if not for her.

Our deepest needs as human beings are to be seen and to be heard. We want to know that we matter! Happiness does not come "someday when . . ." It comes inside ourselves, right now, where we are.

JoAnna Couch

JoAnna Couch is the founder of an executive and employee coaching firm.

Depression can be a sneaky creature. For some of us, it makes a dramatic entrance after a tragic event, a crisis, or a time of grief. For others, it quietly slips into our lives, creating fatigue, self-doubt, and failure.

For me, it was a slow process, and I knew I was there when I found myself as a young mother sitting in the car at red lights and just crying. There were no sad songs on the radio, no sudden sad events in my life, just a sinking feeling of low self-esteem, self-doubt, and finally the realization that my life was not going in the direction I had dreamed it would.

Living without confidence and security was taking its toll on me, manifesting in headaches, stomachaches, fatigue, and a loss of interest in almost everything.

I had bought into the superwoman myth that had become so popular. I was scattered, tired, and out of focus. I wore a fake smile that said, "I'm just great. How are you?"

I just couldn't do it all, yet every woman was told that to be of value, you *had* to do all: work full-time, be the perfect spouse, be the perfect parent, be active and involved at church, serve the community, serve on committees, and so on. It all was supposed to make you a grand and happy person.

One girlfriend suggested we figure out a way to plug Crockpots into the car's cigarette lighter so we could cook while we carpooled!

I sat at red lights and cried because it was the only free time I had, in spite of having a fabulous, supportive husband and wonderful children.

Looking back, I fed right into the lifestyle myths that helped me succumb to depression.

Myth #1: You can have it all.

In the '70s and '80s, women were pushed toward the notion that to be of significance, you needed to earn your space: have a career, pull your share of the load, be a soccer mom who runs a business from the viewing stands of her child's ball game. Don't just enjoy shopping, develop your own import business! A great cook? Start your own catering business. Like to volunteer? Carry a business card that reads "Professional Volunteer."

You were nobody without a business card, and nobody cared if you were running on empty. If you weren't happy, toughen up. You're doing something wrong. Just have it all, baby; have it all.

Myth #2: When things get tough, the tough get going.

Don't feel good about yourself? Then you're not working hard enough! Multitask until you fall into bed totally exhausted. Your significance is only found in your successes. Seize every opportunity. Don't even bother to plan ahead, because life will just get in the way of any plans you happen to make, and you'd better be able to handle it.

Myth #3: When you hit fifty, it's over!

You only have a few years to be all you want to be, so get busy: you're burning daylight! Turning fifty is like standing at the edge of a cliff: Now what? The rest of the world is telling you it's over, you're not attractive anymore, and your services are no longer needed. Are you sitting at red lights with tears in your eyes? Join the club! You have lived long enough to learn that life is not a dress rehearsal after all. It's too late to feel guilty for all the things that didn't go as planned.

Does it have to be this way? Of course not! There are tools you can apply to your own life strategy that will put a smile on your face, a bounce in your stride, and a glow in your heart. But first, you have to take the responsibility. It's up to you—not your children, your friends, your spouse, your extended family, a professor, a pop psychologist, or the economy. It's up to you.

Once you have settled the personal responsibility issue, instead of blaming something or someone else, you're ready to go! My wish for you is that the following tools will be useful to you.

Defeating Myth #1: Create a personal mission statement.

Be the you that God has called you to be. Whether you believe in a divine intelligence or not, it is in your DNA to be pulled toward something greater than yourself. It's that driving force you feel, but you may need a road map to get there.

To help you find your core, your passions, and your strengths, redefine yourself with a personal mission statement. It should reflect who you are, not what you do. Your personal mission statement is like a personal contract that you make with yourself. It will help you focus your energies, make life-changing decisions, and block you from living your life by what others think you should do. You will lead your life based on your personal values and goals. (Use the tips in the sidebar to guide you.)

My mission is to live each day with passion, love, and faith, so I may become closer to God and make a difference in people's lives. I will do this by striving to seek opportunities to engage and help others and by claiming personal study time with inspirational materials. I will develop my practice that is faith-based and future-driven to use my five top strengths that I have developed. I will help others get unstuck, redefine themselves, and reach their full potential.

Defeating Myth #2: Set new boundaries and goals.

Once you have processed this "Who am I?" question using your mission statement, take a long, hard look at what works and what doesn't work for you. We all have boundaries, and when we try to ignore them, we find ourselves swimming upstream.

13

Ask yourself what can be changed, improved, or worked around:

1. What are the financial boundaries in my future?
2. What are my physical limitations?
3. Am I in the best location to develop my mission?
4. Are there educational or certification boundaries?
5. What has not worked well in the past that I need to change?
6. Who inspires me and lifts me up?

Goals are dreams with deadlines. So decide how you want to look and feel six months from now. What do you want to be doing in a year? In five years? Start planning next week, next month, and next year.

Recently, I watched my four-year-old granddaughter work a dot-to-dot picture. As she began to struggle with the next point, she asked herself out loud, "Just what am I making here?" Great question! If she could have seen the whole picture, she could wisely choose her next move. Life is like that. If you do not start with a five-year plan, and bring the focus to this month, your life will be like living dot-to-dot. You won't know what you're making of your life.

Tips for Goal Setting:

1. Be specific and clear. (Not "I want to lose weight," but rather, "I will lose twenty pounds.")
2. They must be written. (Keep these where you can easily glance at them every day.)
3. Set a deadline for each goal. (If you do not set a deadline, there is no way to assess your progress.)
4. Look at the roadblocks. (You can go over, around, under, or through them. Pick the best route.)

5. Ask someone to hold you accountable. (What you're really asking for here is support.)

Defeating Myth #3: Develop your midpoint strategy for significance and satisfaction.

When you look back over your life, you've been busy getting an education, having babies, establishing a home, building a business, climbing the corporate ladder, and doing it all backward and in high heels!

But then something gives you a nudge and says, "What's next?" You're at the midpoint, the period when you take a deep breath and decide if you want to go the rest of the way or regroup and find a better way. You find yourself saying, "Been there, done that. Now what?" Or, "I need better balance in my life." Or, "I've always had a book inside of me."

Deep in your heart, you want to move beyond success. There's more—you can feel it. You are a wise woman with high energy and a heart to help others, but now you need to reframe yourself and shift from focusing on personal achievements to contributing to others.

If you want to stay in the game, it takes planning. This type of planning answers the question, "What's next?" because you want to respond to that driving force in you. Therefore you set about planning how to use your experiences, finances, strengths, passions, and resources to live with a new purpose. There may be adjustments, especially in finding the right vehicle to do what you were called to do. It may call for some sacrifices to get in your mode. I believe that we were created to do a work that God has intended us to do. It's a driving force inside of each of us.

Women of all ages find themselves wading through a swamp of myths. These were the three myths that stuck to the bottom of *my* soul like gum on the sole of a shoe. It took wise mentors to help me make a shift and scrape off the goo.

My husband lifted me and encouraged me. My own personal coach called me to accountability. Your myths and challenges may look a little different, but the basic tools for loving your life and living intentionally are there for you to use.

JoAnna Couch—Create Your Personal Mission Statement

For an in-depth exercise and other suggestions visit www.FranklinCovey.com. Here are a few quick suggestions to get you started:

- **Draw a map of where you have been.** List all major events, decisions, circumstances, and ideas you have had that brought you to where you are today. Use words, pictures, and symbols. Look for strengths you have developed and skills you have acquired.

- **Think of how you want the future to look.** Is there something that is calling you in a certain direction? A passion you have? Put this into words. Keep it simple, clear, and brief—five or six sentences. Can you link strengths from the past to the wise woman you are today?

- **Focus on your personal belief system.** Who do you want to become in the coming years? What do you want your character to be? Write this down, too. Your statement should include actions and qualities that will have an impact for years to come. When these change, you will change.

- **Consider the emotional and eternal "payoff."** This exercise will help you in the coming years. For example, pull this statement out when you're stuck on a decision. Will saying yes or making a certain choice enrich this person you are becoming? Does it support the mission you are on? If not, say no.

Sherri's Tips:
Renew Your Emotional Energy

- **Take breaks.** Take breaks frequently. Get up and stretch, take the dog for a walk, play catch, or go for a walk to clear your mind and soul.
- **Take a "staycation."** Our hometowns have so much to offer; take a vacation at home and enjoy the sights.
- **Tune out.** Turn off your phone, put away your laptop, and be still.
- **Choose happiness.** You can choose your responses, look on the bright side, and see the opportunities.
- **Accept yourself as you are.** You can improve your looks and your attitude with good nutrition, exercise, and clear thinking.
- **Silence your critic.** Notice the good things around you instead of focusing on what's wrong.
- **Practice gratitude.** Happy people are grateful for what they have. Unhappy people just want more and more and are never satisfied.
- **Dump toxic clutter.** Eliminate social clutter such as toxic or emotionally draining relationships. Just like emptying your wastebasket allows you to start fresh, make room for relationships that nourish your soul.
- **Lighten up.** Don't let little things ruin your day. Don't expect perfection from others or yourself.
- **Enjoy the moment.** Time with your family, your spouse, and your friends is precious. We don't know how long we have on this earth, so make what you have count.

Well done, my good and faithful servant. You have been faithful in handling this small amount, so now I will give you many more responsibilities. Let's celebrate together!
—Matthew 25:23 NLT

2

Unexpected
Roadblocks

"When we come to the end of the
light we know, and are about to step off
into the darkness of the unknown,
of this we can be sure . . . either God
will provide something solid to stand on
or we will be taught to fly."
—Author Unknown

Acts of God, acts of will, and acts-a-dents can all change the course of your life and send you in a direction you don't want to go. If you don't like where you are at this point in your life, there's probably plenty of blame to pass around, but what's the point? If you want to get back on track, or set a new course, it's up to one person and one person only: you! You're the one who has to make changes before you can influence anyone or anything else.

Sherri Elliott-Yeary

Most of us long to create a future that is fulfilling and inspiring. We spend countless hours dreaming about the day when our goals will be satisfied and our hearts content. "Will this choice bring me long-term fulfillment or will it bring me short-term gratification?" is a vital question for all of us who are committed to turning our dreams into realities. Staying focused on long-term desires is essential as we go about our day-to-day activities because it's easy to get sidetracked and experience a momentary lapse in memory just as we're about to move powerfully toward our desired goals. When we ask this question before we make a choice, we are able to tell if we are choosing to stay on the path of our dreams or take a detour from our desired direction.

To have long-term fulfillment, we must stand in the vision for our future. It takes a certain amount of tenacity and focus to stay on course. It's human nature to opt for the quick fix, preferring to suffer the consequences of our behavior later. Our momentary desires often win out over our commitments to the future and living the life we are supposed to live.

Choices made in the heat of the moment, without thought of the consequences, are choices based on instant gratification. They come unannounced, usually in the form of a compulsion, an impulse, or a craving. They can sneak up on us unexpectedly. When we make choices responding to an urge, an impulse, or a whim, we can be certain they are based on instant gratification rather than long-term fulfillment.

As I was preparing for this chapter of the book, I was reminded of a conversation with a girlfriend who stated, "Every once in a while I just wish my life would unfold normally like everyone else's." I knew the feeling, but I quickly responded, "Normal? There's no such thing as normal!"

Looking in from the outside, it may seem like someone else's life is easier than yours, but it isn't. Life happens differently for everyone.

When I left my corporate role as VP of HR and risk for a national staffing firm over seven years ago, I made the choice that if I was going to work so hard, it would be on my terms with my clients. I wanted to educate employers on the value of their employees and how critical it is they "walk the talk" in their roles as leaders.

I discovered my skills and abilities allowed me the opportunity to provide the services I was passionate about and still make a good living as a consultant. Just prior to the official launch of my first book, I was approached by an international staffing firm to speak at their national conference at the Gaylord Texan Hotel in Dallas. I agreed, even though I had never spoken in front of a large audience before other than in my role as a trainer in HR.

Providing a keynote speech is very different than engaging and motivating a smaller audience, as I was about to discover. In fact, I hadn't planned to become a speaker and was secretly afraid to speak in front of a larger group. I realized sometimes things are put in front of you, and it's up to you to take the challenge and climb the mountain or not.

One area of my training specialties is generational differences in the workplace, so I prepared for the event like a good trainer would do, by studying the most current generational issues, especially with the growing need for expanded talent acquisition, advances in new technologies, and staffing changes due to the economic downturn.

I sent my speech to the special events director per her request for review, but what she did was share it with her company's internal marketing person, who happened to be scheduled to speak ahead of me on the topic of staffing trends. This speaker used the majority of my researched material in her speech, and spoke twenty minutes into my allotted time!

I was suddenly faced with having to alter my speech on the spot at the last minute. As I took the podium and looked into the eyes of each audience member, total fear enveloped me. Since I was not a professional speaker, I had my handwritten notes clutched in my left hand and felt blindsided and nervous, but I began. The microphone was placed on the right side of my jacket, so every time I got nervous and swiped my paper across my chest, a loud boom came out of the microphone repeatedly. Did I emphasis the word *repeatedly?*

It was my first big appearance as a speaker, and I did what many of us women would do. I invited my best girlfriends, co-workers, partners, etc., including my good friends and authors Sandra Yancey (eWomen Network), and Nancy Barry (author and motivational speaker). Not only was I bad, but I was bad in front of my closest friends and other accomplished authors. I felt like I had let them down.

A few days after the event, I received neither a thank you nor an apology from the staffing firm, but instead got a scathing e-mail chastising me for being late with my speech, keeping people too long, and not having anything original to share. My lack of "polish" in my presentation was a mark on their reputation for having chosen me as a speaker.

When I accepted the speaking opportunity, I did so without pay, so I was upset to say the least, but instead of dwelling on the anger and embarrassment, I realized I had a lot to learn about being a speaker and set my focus on this new challenge.

The previous summer, I had the opportunity to listen to a dynamic speaker who presented for Sandra Yancey's eWomen conference. Her name is Alecia Huck and she is the CEO of her own marketing firm. She dominated the stage and kept us engaged and entertained for the entire hour. I called Sandra, who is a friend and a client, and asked for a referral to Alecia. Due to Sandra's connection, I was able to get Alecia to work with me on improving my presentation, speaking skills, and confidence to stand up in front of an audience.

Alecia graciously listened to me recount my story of terror and shame during my previous speech. We both had a good laugh—or maybe I cried (I am not sure, but probably both). We set a date for her to come from Denver to visit me in Dallas so we could work together in person.

While I presented to a new group, Alecia sat in the back of the room and took plenty of notes as she watched me. Then we spent the next day refining my message and style. She had me speak again, and we refined it again. During this process, Alecia treated me with kindness and respect while showing me that I had it within me to be a great speaker. I'll forever be indebted to her.

Over the last few years, I've had the privilege to really grow the speaking side of my business, even speaking internationally. I am so grateful I had the internal drive, determination, and fire to overcome my fear of public speaking and authentically share myself with audiences.

Now I coach others on how to overcome obstacles and roadblocks as they develop their message and overcome challenges to achieve their dreams. My motivation every time I take the podium is to move, touch, and inspire my audience. If I can do that, then I have delivered on my promise to the audience and to myself.

Karla K. Morton

2010 Texas Poet Laureate

My whole life I longed to be Texas's Poet Laureate. I told my mom when I was a little girl that that was what I wanted to be when I grew up. Then, one day much later, I was nominated.

On May 19, 2008, I got the call that changed my life—but it wasn't the one I was hoping for.

Driving home with a new eighty-pound canine companion,

I answered the phone. It was my doctor calling to tell me the results of my breast biopsy. I didn't even make it into the house; I just sat on the porch, crying. I had cancer and needed to start aggressive treatment right away. My new, very large dog crawled up into my lap and we sat like that for a long time, this dog and I who had only known each other for a mere two hours.

His name was Pontus, a Scottish deerhound. He joined Butterfinger, a stray cat who claimed us, and they

24

both kept me company while I underwent surgery, chemotherapy, and radiation. I've thought many times that God answers our prayers before we even know what we need, and my pets proved his graciousness during this time.

When I wrote *Redefining Beauty* in 2008 I was writing to get myself through it, to deal with the wounds and scars that the cancer caused, to try to manage the fear. I did not realize I was writing a manuscript. I was simply raging against the disease by writing. The book, as it became, provided me an avenue to express my feelings and emotions during that difficult period.

We've been conditioned since childhood that beauty is what we see—physical beauty—and the things that "make" a woman are her hair and breasts. Those are the very two things a woman loses when she has breast cancer, requiring much soul searching to redefine her idea of beauty.

Since then, my whole idea of beauty has changed. Most people perceive the desert as being hot and colorless, but when you strip it down, natural "beauty" is a rock. It's that one solid thing that is your true essence. It doesn't matter what surrounds you, like a colorless desert. Your essence is beautiful. When you find your core beauty like that, there is nothing anyone can do or say that will make you feel differently.

Cancer is a kick in the gut, but the hardest thing is the fear; it's a reaction that paralyzes. When a friend said this profound statement, "I don't think you can have complete fear and complete faith at the same time," I chose not to be afraid.

Fighting the fear was a mental battle, so I pulled on my cowboy boots every day, wore the biggest earrings I could find, and told myself, "You're not going down without a fight." If I was going to participate in my own healing, it would have to start in my mind.

I chose to increase my faith. And knowing that God wants only the best for me changed things.

I used writing as an instrument in my healing. The paper can take it if you're angry. If you want to put your fist through the wall, write it down! It takes some pressure off and provides great therapy. Besides, paper is more easily replaceable than drywall. I also chose to laugh through the fight and decided that I was protected one way or another; God's hand was on me.

Was my faith rewarded? Yes. Faith can minimize our troubles. With faith, you are allowed to say, "I will physically do what I can and throw my hands up in the air for the rest." For those of us who are extremely driven people, it's hard to "rearrange life." It's hard to loosen the reins and say, "There's a stronger power at work here, and He has my goodness at heart. Let Him do his job."

Part of my challenge in that is learning how to rest. Women tend to want to do it all and take care of everything, leaving little time for rest. Take the time to say, "I've done what I can do, so now I'll take a nap." Let God work through *the rest*. He has your best interests at heart.

When I was a kid, I would go to the back pasture where I felt that the wind had something to tell me, and if I listened long enough, I would be able to understand. We should all give ourselves permission to rest, listen, and have downtime. That's not wasting time; it's a time of renewal. My power, strength, and rejuvenation come from rest.

Many of us operate in survivor mode: get the kids to school, go to work, pick them up, cook dinner, put them in baths, and fall into bed exhausted. There's no time left to enjoy the world around us.

Having to go through chemotherapy and radiation is physically exhausting. But I rest by getting a cup of tea and going outside. It's there that I feel like a child again with the touch of the sun on my face. I listen to the wind. I'll sit in the shade and think, *I'm amazed at the number of leaves in the trees or that the bird has only one song—but it's glorious.* I'm awed by the glory of the world. Now my cancer is gone and I'm choosing to live my life a new way. I'm fortunate they found my cancer early, that it hadn't spread, and that they were able to take care of it.

My message to you, the reader, is this: *we already have it all.* You have to choose to look at your life like that: you are already so blessed and there are things that you do so well. You're superwoman. There is a strength that is only yours. You need those quiet moments to discover yourself.

Find the thing that brings you joy, whatever replenishes you. (For me, it's being outside.) Don't feel guilty about it; it's as important as anything else in your life. Give yourself permission to rest and then claim those moments for yourself. Enjoy *not* working. And let the healing begin.

Author's note: Exactly one year later, on May 19, 2009, Karla got the call she'd been waiting for: she had been chosen as the 2010 Texas Poet Laureate.

Gail Penry
Retired Marketing Executive

Sometimes you don't get to have it all: you don't get to have your health. We're all doing more with less, but I've had to learn how to live with less income due to forced retirement. You can either live on a whole lot of money, or you can live on nothing.

I was diagnosed with lupus while I was still working, but there was no forgiveness in my workforce. I was working in the assisted living industry. I was the admissions and marketing director, gave tours, did the admissions paperwork, and I dealt with the family when there were issues. I was also taking care of an elderly aunt, and my boss fired me because I wasn't completely available. I was only 0.5 percent from my sales goal when I was fired.

I saw the writing on the wall and filed for disability. You have to wait two years for Medicare after being approved for disability. To live on disability, you have to go through a process to get approved. I believe the Social Security Administration has an actuary look at your disease. They hope you'll die because it will cost them less over time. I was determined to live.

Lupus is an autoimmune disease. It ebbs and flows; I have good days and bad days. On bad days, I feel like I'm on fire. Sometimes my body just won't go; I can't make it move. On good days, I can call a friend to visit, but I'm not as reliable anymore. People can't count on me, because I don't know how I'm going to feel on any particular day. If you're not in touch with anybody, the social isolation makes you feel even worse.

Sometimes I wake up in tears. Most people don't understand; they have too much going on in their own lives to think about a chronically ill person. Cancer they can understand, but lupus they don't understand. With most autoimmune diseases, like MS, where the body is attacking itself, people don't understand the severity of the disease because you may look "fine" when they see you.

What they don't know is that you've saved your strength, sometimes for days, and propped yourself up with meds just to be able to meet them for dinner. You get to where you don't make plans but you can have fun on the spur of the moment.

To make life livable, I have pets, and—when I feel like it—I do a lot of political work, like letter-writing and awareness campaigns. It stimulates my mind. I do volunteer work for candidates, and I've found there is a lot I can do, which makes me feel useful, needed, and wanted. I send a lot of "awareness" e-mails:

"Are you aware that this or that is happening?" I was determined to stay connected to the outside world even if I was stuck indoors due to my disease.

My aunt passed away and left me a little money, which I used to turn my house into a home. By doing so, I made it more comfortable, more "mine," more replenishing. I now love my home and the neighborhood where the cats and I live. Love what you have, have what you need, be happier with less.

Sherri's Tips:
Positive Ways to Reframe Your Situation

Have you ever noticed that two people can face the same situation and one person describes it as a harrowing ordeal while another views it as a minor inconvenience? Or have you had one of those days when everything seems to be going wrong until you hear about someone else's troubles that make yours pale in comparison? Have you ever faced a challenge in your life that initially seemed negative, but something so positive came out of it that you're glad it happened? These situations all involve a phenomenon that psychologists refer to as reframing.

What is reframing?
Reframing is a method of changing the way you look at something, which changes the way you experience it. It's a way that we can alter our perceptions of stressors and thus relieve significant amounts of stress to create more positive outcomes.

Reframing makes a stressful event easier to bear simply by affecting your attitude and response. It can turn a major trauma into a challenge to be bravely overcome. Reframing can depict a really bad day as a mildly low point in an overall wonderful life and turn a negative event into a valuable learning experience.

How does reframing affect stress?

Using reframing techniques can actually change your physical responses to stress because your body's stress response is triggered by *perceived* stress, not actual events.

If you perceive you are threatened—physically or psychologically—by a situation, your "fight or flight" response will kick in. Your stress response can be triggered by events ranging from annoying to frightening, and can remain triggered long after the event has passed, especially if you're not practicing relaxation techniques.

How can reframing work for you?

Reframing techniques can help you minimize the perceived stressors in your life, allowing you to respond calmly and reasonably. It prevents you from overreacting or spending your energies in areas that won't improve the situation. Instead, you can preserve your energy and direct it toward appropriate responses and solutions. Using reframing techniques can be simple and easy, especially with practice.

Learn about thinking patterns.

Since pessimists tend to experience more stress and less success than optimists, it's important to understand the differences in how they think. Educating yourself about thinking patterns is important to laying the groundwork for understanding and change. Is your glass half-empty or half-full?

Notice your thoughts.

Learn to recognize when you're slipping into overly negative and stress-inducing patterns of thinking. The proof is in the results: if you feel weak or inadequate to the challenges of daily life, you're probably handicapping yourself with negative thoughts.

Challenge your thoughts.

As you notice your negative thoughts, examine the truth and accuracy (or lack thereof) of these thoughts. Are the things you're telling yourself even true? Are there other ways to interpret the same set of events? Which ways of seeing things serves you better? Your thoughts should fit your situation, but reflect a more positive outlook.

Replace stinkin' thinkin'.

When you're looking at a negative situation, see if you can change your own self-talk to empower yourself and others. Reframe a setback into a learning opportunity. Look for the gift in each situation, and see if you can move your stressors to the more positive edge of reality.

Reframing can have a huge impact on your stressors. Changing the way you look at your life can truly *change* your life!

> *"We can make our plans, but the Lord determines our steps."*
> —*Proverbs 16:9* NLT

3

Moments
of
Choice

"Everyone thinks of changing the world, but
no one thinks of changing himself."
—Leo Tolstoy

I have a plaque in my office that states "Change is hard—you go first."
First we must understand the choices that inspire and motivate us, then
make the necessary changes to achieve the life we desire. If it were easy,
everyone would do it. But that's what makes you special: you can adapt and
grow. It's just a matter of confidence and deciding where to best focus your
efforts. In your pursuit to have it all, but not all at once, what can you do
with the twenty-four hours you have each day? What's taking too much of
your time and energy?

It's time to rebalance the tires of your life, learn to accept what you can't
change, and work smarter—not harder—on the things you can change.

Sherri Elliott-Yeary

Every day, each of us makes a multitude of choices that will impact our lives. Some of these choices are minor and will only impact the next few minutes, hours, or days, while others will completely change the direction of our lives. Some choices are easy to make; some are more difficult. Some will lead us straight to success, while others will bring us face-to-face with failure. Some seem completely insignificant. But what's imperative for each of us to know is that, no matter how large or small, easy or difficult, each choice we make, individually or collectively, alters the direction of our lives. The quality of our choices will dictate whether we will struggle in frustration or live an extraordinary life—the life of our dreams.

Our ability to make choices implies certain rights and freedoms. If we can choose, we can determine which decisions we will make about our bodies, our health, our relationships, our finances, our careers, our social lives, and our spiritual beliefs. Choice allows us to pick between paths and make the change. To go right or left. To move forward or backward, be happy or sad, loving or hateful, satisfied or discontent. Choice gives us the power to be successful or unfulfilled, to be good or great, and to feel pleasure or pain. We can keep busy or slow down, be faithful, be disciplined, or be lazy. We can pursue a path that reflects our highest selves or one that reflects our lowest selves. Ultimately, we are the ones who get to choose.

What distinguishes us from all other forms of life is our capacity to weigh our options and make conscious, deliberate changes. The ability to make choices just might be our most precious gift.

Today is based on the choices and changes we made yesterday, three days ago, three months ago, and three years ago. We don't wind up fifty thousand dollars in debt because of one choice. We don't put on thirty unwanted pounds as a result of two poor diet choices. And our relationships usually don't fall apart overnight because of one bad decision. We are where we are because of repeated subconscious or unhealthy choices that we've made day after day that add up to the reality we find ourselves in. If we want to understand why and how we created our present reality, all we need to do is look at the choices we made in the past. Examining our present circumstances will show us that we got where we are as a result of decisions we made yesterday and the days before that.

Most of us have lost sight of the relationship between our choices, our actions, and their outcomes. Instead of taking responsibility for our current state of affairs, we become masters at assigning blame, pretending that everything is someone else's fault when our lives turn out not to be the wonderlands we want them to be. We point fingers at others instead of looking at the choices we've made that have landed us exactly where we are today. Without bringing conscious awareness to our choices, we can't help but repeat the patterns of our past.

When I married Mason, I knew he was a gift from God. He is the love of my life. I knew I needed to make corrections and adjustments in my priorities to live the life we wanted. Mason is the sweetest, most generous man and he has an abundance of patience. Thank you, Lord.

My book tour for *Ties to Tattoos* kept me on the road an average of two hundred and fifty days per year. If I wanted to have a healthy marriage and spend time with Mason, I needed to change how and where I worked. All of the sudden my world was upside down; I no longer wanted to travel for my work 90 percent of the time. I missed being home with my husband and family. It became evident after much thought and prayer that my decisions and the choices I made in the future would also impact our life together as a couple.

This was a revelation for me to think as a married woman, not as a single business professional. That moment of clarity allowed me to understand how my decisions impacted my new commitment to a healthy and happy personal life. Yes, it was different, but change is not hard when you powerfully choose to embrace the change and are all in!

The path of success clearly presents itself when you make yourself available to hear the message.

April Vaughn-Donovan
Owner of Snelling Staffing Services in North Texas

A lot of my story is about breaking free of addiction—things in life that drag me down. I was working a corporate job that had me traveling frequently; I was in a verbally and physically abusive marriage; I had two small children at home; and I was miserable.

I spent a lot of time on my knees in prayer: "God, I'm alone, and my children have seen things they shouldn't have seen, and now I don't know what to do. Help me figure this out."

It was a desire for independence. When you come through a relationship with an abusive partner, it's a hard life to imagine. He didn't want me too independent or to know that I had options. I wanted to be independent and make my own rules.

I decided to completely change everything about my life. In a three-week period, I left my corporate job of ten years, separated from my abusive husband, and started a new business sixty miles away from my home with the kids.

When I graduated from college, I immediately went to work for a national staffing firm. So when I decided to slow life down years later, the franchise sales executive suggested that Sherman, Texas, would be a good place to start my business. I got some financial backing from my mom and stepfather and left my corporate pay and benefits behind for a place where I had no roots. I would meet my mom and stepfather at the gas station and grocery store where they would pay for my gas and food. It was a struggle, but it felt right. Eighteen months later, I was still commuting because I couldn't sell my house in Allen, Texas. Sixty miles between my children and my new office was just too far. I was exhausted with the startup and trying to keep the house clean for showings. It was stressful.

So I bought a travel trailer, and the kids and I left; we moved from a 2,500 square foot home to a trailer and lived there for an entire summer. Downsizing teaches you a lot about what your real needs are and what your personal wants are.

When I built my new office, I made a special room for my children so I could spend as much time with them as possible. They had computers, toys, and their own couch. We'd leave the office at 5:00 p.m., go home to the trailer, put on our swimsuits, and go to the lake and eat dinner on a raft. It was the most wonderful summer of my life. After four and a half months passed, the house in Allen finally sold and we were able to buy a house in Sherman that backs up to a cow pasture.

I had made all kinds of changes, but it was time to address the elephant still left in the room: my weight. I had to ask myself, *Why do I weigh 330 pounds?* There's something wrong here. I had peeled away the layers to get through these life changes, and it was time to face the fact that I was addicted to food in an unhealthy way.

Losing weight is not just about counting calories; you have to get your emotions in check and get yourself emotionally whole. What's so strange is that my defense mechanism was an overinflated self-confidence. No one knew that my weight bothered me. People who don't have a weight problem have healthy relationships with food, but it made me feel weak, lazy and flawed. So I protected myself by thinking, *I'm owning it. I may be 330 pounds, but I have fabulous shoes and earrings.*

I had to get my mind around it. I got lap-band surgery, and it took off sixty pounds. But when my weight hit a plateau, I realized that surgery is just a tool. You have to change everything; by seeking God, I lost the remaining seventy pounds through diet and exercise. But first, I had to get rid of the baggage in my life.

My mom and stepfather raised me, and I hadn't seen my biological father since I was ten years old. One day, my biological father showed up unannounced and said, "I want to be in your life." I hadn't seen him for twenty-five years. He's a successful businessman in the Hill Country, but I never really had the chance to get to know him as my father. Once I had the chance to get to know him, he reinforced a lot of good things that I already knew about myself.

My husband, Sean, is a gift from God. He is fifteen years older than me and has no kids, but he took on my children. "It's never *your* children, it's *our* children," he'd say. I just don't know many who can do that with such grace.

He is the kindest, most beautiful person I have ever met. He is a supervisor in a factory, a blue-collar guy. He proposed to me when I was 330 pounds. I don't need anything from Sean financially; the only thing I need is love. When you strip it down to that, it's not complicated. His love makes me feel so much more secure, which has a lot to do with healing the inside so I can work on the outside.

I've been struggling with depression because of my parents; they've been going through a divorce and have done horrible things to each other. My stepfather stole a bunch of money from my company and left my mom ten days after my grandmother died. My mom broke into his apartment and gave him sleep medicine so he would sleep while she went through his cell phone. He ended up going to the emergency room. My stepfather is now on girlfriend number five. They're both lucky they're not in jail for all of their issues. What drama!

This was all unbelievable to me. I grew up in a rainbow and unicorn world. We were socialites in Louisiana. My stepfather is an oil man and put me through college. Now he's drained my business. We were able to right our cash flow, but the money he took should have paid down our debt. Our padding is gone.

I need to find myself again. I'm going through all this yuck; I long to detoxify myself, appreciate what God gave us, and re-connect with the realness in the world—not the superficial stuff.

So I'm going back to the travel trailer. My girlfriends, children, and I are going to Yellowstone National Park for two weeks to just get away. I've never done anything like this before, and my husband asked, "Who does that?" I said, "I do." Sean was totally supportive of my need for emotional renewal.

When I'm in pain, the travel trailer is a place I go; it takes me where I want to go. I showed up in this town six years ago and didn't know anyone. I feel like I have had the gift of all these people who have invested in me and my business, and it's an amazing feeling to take with me on this journey.

If you had told me a week ago that I would be driving a ten thousand pound trailer, I would have said, "You're crazy!" But I'm doing it and God will show me the beauty I've lost touch with. The old April will be back soon, with her pink bling and sassiness.

Jan West Tardy

Protocol, Etiquette and Image Consultant, and Speaker

If you would like to see a picture of change, just send me your address through my website, and I will send you photos of myself as a young woman and as the woman I am today. Frankly,

as I look at my photos, I can see that my freckles have turned into age spots and my dishwater blonde hair is now sterling silver, or as my brother says, "Old gray mare hair." But those aren't the changes that matter most. What matters is what happened to change me on the inside.

I grew up on a farm. My parents were not financially well off, but my childhood was golden. My mother was, and is, a beautiful woman. She was pampered and protected from birth and spent most of her life concerned about her own well-being. My father cherished her, and we all played our parts in following his lead.

My father was charismatic and adventurous. I thought he was probably the most handsome and smartest man on earth. We had people at our home all the time. Friends or family would be outside playing baseball or inside playing cards. As children, my siblings and I spent our time exploring, building clubhouses, and creating fun. We had Shetland ponies, a pond, swings, and the homes of our friends were a few miles down the dirt road each direction.

Sometimes, late at night, my daddy would get all of us up and into our station wagon. We would drive through the pastures with our headlights on and greyhounds leading the way, bounding over ruts and grasses in pursuit of coyotes. Not the safest of circumstances, but for a child, they were certainly the most exciting.

When it rained and we could not work on the farm, we would be packed and in the car at any hour, day or night, to head to the mountains. I wish I had a nickel for all the times I woke up to my father yelling, "Rise and shine!"

Even though money was tight, my father was generous to a fault. In fact, money that we needed as a family was always given to someone if they asked him for help. I never realized until I was an adult how broke we really were in the early days. As a teenager, when I wanted money, Daddy would say, "We have all the money you need, spend what you want." Or, he would say, "We're broke, don't spend anything." I learned from his variety of responses that money may come or go, but it should not change who you are or who your friends are; it should only change your spending habits.

My father was killed two weeks before my nineteenth birthday and the world as I knew it came to an end. When I learned about my father's death, I literally prayed to make the world stop while sobbing on the floor in my brother's bathroom. And so, for me, it did. I could not move forward, make any decisions, or leave my bedroom without moving in a daze and crying. I felt guilt, anger, depression, and every other negative emotion that you might imagine. I could not accept this change in my life.

Then, one day, I began to think about my father himself instead of the effect his passing had on me. He was an eternal optimist, energetic, and full of life; I knew he would not be happy seeing me so miserable. I had to move in some direction.

So I got married.

I should point out that when your life changes in a dramatic way, it's not a good idea to make lifelong commitments. You should take the time to get yourself right first. Jumping into a situation thinking that someone else will make everything better is not only unrealistic, it is downright wrong. But that's what I did.

My first marriage was wrong from the beginning. My husband never seemed happy with me. I worked on myself to try to improve on a daily basis so I could please him. I learned how to work hard physically and mentally to try to prove myself worthy of the marriage. After all, I was brought up in a happy family situation and believed that if you got married, you stayed married. I felt I needed to be what he wanted me to be. I was a model of change. But not all change is right.

Shortly after my fortieth birthday, my husband decided *he* needed a change. He was quite sure he had never loved me in the twenty-plus years of our marriage, and he wanted out. Once again, I spent the next several months moving in a daze and crying.

42

After a while, my thoughts turned away from grief and back on what really mattered. I thought about how blessed I was in so many ways, and I thought about my two beautiful children. I also believed that if I did not change, it would make me a loser and my ex-husband a winner. I did not want to be a loser.

I decided that I could not alter the way he felt or who he was, but I was free to be whatever or whoever I wanted. I opted for being strong and happy and moving forward.

Luckily, all those years of trying to please someone else paid off in unexpected ways. For me, change had become a way of life. I left the marriage with only a little college education and no job in sight, but without fear of change. Every job I took after that point was one I had no knowledge of prior to taking it, but I knew I could learn what I needed to know to be a good worker. Living with someone for twenty years and trying to be "perfect" enough for them to love you will teach you how to work hard, if nothing else.

The first job was bookkeeping and managing computers for an insurance company. Forget that I had never worked on insurance books or worked at all on a computer. I could type some, and I was good at math. How hard could it be? I think I had been at the company about a week when I accidentally shut down the whole office because I did *not* know how to work computers. I got an education that day! I managed to do a great job for the company, but I needed more. I decided to go back to school for a "real" education and a degree.

While in college, I was hired to do a tax audit for a large corporation. I might mention here that I knew nothing about taxes or audits, but why would that be a problem? I just set my mind to it; fortunately, the audit went well. I learned that people skills will help you in any situation and auditors are people too. I managed to save the company a lot of money and even received an award.

My life changed dramatically when I remarried and graduated from college. My second marriage was great from the start and continues to be one of the best life changes to come my way. My husband is loving and supportive and thinks I am beautiful! It feels wonderful. It is funny, but I will be forever grateful to my first husband for giving me no option to save our marriage. It was a forced change that allowed me to learn, grow, and marry the nicest, kindest, most handsome man I know!

Graduating from college was life-changing because it meant I had finally finished something. Finishing something you start is a good thing. I graduated with a business degree just one semester before my daughter graduated from college. Small victories are sweet.

Over the next several years, there were many work-related changes as I went to work for my husband. Crop insurance sales, insurance office management, and real estate sales were the fields chosen for me.

Change isn't always your choice, but jumping into each new job knowing that change could be good and anything could be learned was all I needed to understand. Each job, even if it wasn't suited to me, provided a wealth of knowledge and a wonderful growth experience.

Not being comfortable in a job can sometimes lead to good changes, and that was what happened next. My husband and I decided to move away from our small town and start following our passions in a vital growing community near Austin, Texas. He loves commercial real estate and is successfully doing that full-time.

I had a passion too. I decided to make the world a more civil place, one person at a time. While working in the residential real estate market, I was shocked by the fact that people did not always act like professionals. Unreturned calls, inappropriate dress, and arrogant attitudes by agents were the norm. I began to wonder what had happened to common courtesies. Watching people in restaurants attack their food or lean over plates like they are guarding property made me realize that table manners are no longer taught at home. Cell phone usage in restaurants, on streets, in cars, and in stores is out of control. Sloppy dress at work, school, and in public denotes a lack of regard for those around us. Sales clerks no longer understand that greeting and servicing clients are what keep paychecks coming.

I decided to try to change those habits that have taken us away from the social graces and begin to create a more civil world. Not only could I help promote change in those around me, I could improve myself!

This was the best change because it was the one I most valued and believed in and was the first work-related change I actually chose to make! This career brought about a new goal and mission. It's time to create a more civil world—and positive, uplifting changes are always good.

One of my most memorable experiences in the new field was helping a young chief operating officer of a thriving business with his dining etiquette. We had such fun and he left with a new confidence about work-related social events. But the best part was that when he went home, he and his wife sat with their children at a formal dining table and went over all the skills he had learned. He said it was a great experience with his family; they laughed, learned, and changed together!

Another experience involved the use of social media. A friend who is beautiful, smart, and beginning her own business is also a body builder. Her goal was to use Facebook to promote her business as a life coach geared toward corporations.

Unfortunately, she used a photo in which she was scantily dressed as her profile photo. I did not know this until I tried to get a friend of mine to look seriously at her for some corporations she represented. My corporate friend took one look at her Facebook photo and dismissed her entirely. My young friend was surprised when I called to tell her what happened and suggested that she change the photo. This is a great example of why our profiles on social websites need correct protocol.

My beautiful mother passed away only recently. While my whole life has been about change, my mother's life has been spent trying to avoid it. "Change your diet" and "change your lifestyle" were words she did not want to hear. Things always came easily for her, and she was used to getting her way without having to change anything. She lived out her final days angry and confused. She didn't look like she wanted to look, and her body wouldn't do what she wanted it to do anymore. She hated being helpless.

Most of us don't have the luxury of being supported, loved, and protected like my mother did. We have to change if we want to get what we want out of life.

Hopefully you will take time to look into my eyes in the photos, if you request them. I still have a little youthful spark there, and the laugh lines are well-earned. I now see the beauty of all the blessings that life has brought. Also, my smile is much as it was, only a little more sincere now, or more knowing. And even though you can't see it in the photo, my heart is much bigger and a lot softer. A more tolerant person exists in the second photo, one totally changed by faith, life, love, and work.

My father's death made me understand the value of life. My divorce and remarriage taught me that you can't make someone love you, but there are people who will love you without having to change who you are. My work experiences taught me how to learn, grow, and find confidence in my abilities. My mother's life and passing taught me that change is hard when you don't welcome it. My family has taught me what it is to love uncondi-tionally, and God has given me faith to move forward knowing the best is yet to be.

Now, it's your turn. Find photos of a young and old "you" or look at yourself in the mirror and think back. How were you then and how are you after all the changes in your life, whether chosen or not chosen by you? Your reflection will tell you how you have handled life's changes. Are you angry? Hard? Do you often ask, "Why me?" and hold pity parties? Or have you learned to go to your knees and ask for help? Are you softer? More gentle? Do you ask, "How do I adjust?" and "What lesson is to be learned?" or "How can knowing what I know help someone else in the same situation?" Are you a problem-solver and a solutions-finder? Do you take one step forward even if it means two steps back? Do you welcome new beginnings?

A divorce, a death, a layoff, or a move are just a few of the things that can nail your foot to the floor and make you go in circles. The first thing you have to do is find the hammer and pry the nail out so you can take that first step forward, painful as it might be. The greatest joys can come from the deepest hurts, but it takes making those first steps to work through the pain and make your way to the joy.

If you have the ability to look in the mirror it means that you are alive and change is inevitable. If it is not the reflection you want to see, then ask yourself how you are going to deal with change from this point forward. Change is coming whether you like it or not, so learn to like it.

Change can be hard, but with faith it can bring you to a better place. Change is life; make a decision to live it.

Kathy Garland

Management Effectiveness Coach and Speaker

I have found that sometimes life creates balance for you. I haven't found the perfect balance and have come to realize part of the game is to be happy with where I am. The more I focus on what is wrong and not working, the more I feel out of balance.

My eighty-seven-year-old father recently died. During his illness and hospitalizations, family was first. I will never regret the time I spent with my father or the times I helped my mother. It was the right thing for me to do. During this period, I didn't get to see my friends and other family as much. Luckily, with close family and good friends, you can pick up where you left off at any time.

I did lose some business opportunities and revenue because I wanted to be with my parents. I was OK with that. The good thing is that with focus and reestablishing priorities, I was able to get back on track. Everything is a choice. The more conscious I am about my choices, the more I sense peace or balance.

Now I'm back at work full force; my priorities have shifted again. Am I more balanced? Hard to say; this is where I am right now. I am doing what is most important, and that is what balance means to me. I've learned that if I stay present to what I'm doing, I at least feel more balanced and less stressed.

Life-changing events immediately shift your priorities. The importance of everything else fades. How you handle your priorities and how you react during difficult circumstances help you during times when life is "normal" (if there is such a thing).

I've experienced life-altering events such as having children, changing jobs, losing jobs, moving across the country, and living in another country. These transitional times in my life were opportunities for me to reflect upon and reevaluate my priorities and interests.

In the last five years, I've taken many steps to improve my life, including consulting with a nutritionist, changing my diet, and joining a health club. I also worked with a personal trainer and took martial arts lessons. I have pushed myself into uncomfortable areas, like going on a giant swing over a deep canyon and taking assignments that were a big stretch. I led an annual women's retreat for over four years and got my management coaching effectiveness certification so I could understand others and myself better.

Success takes focus, intention, and faith, but mistakes can happen when you take your eyes off the target. I'd say that if anyone is having trouble "having it all" they have too many priorities, and need to learn how to narrow their focus and say no. It's a lesson I'm still learning.

Sherri's Tips:
Choices and Change

- **Don't just do something; sit there.** If you're facing a massive rescaling of your life, your first impulse will be to go into a whirling spin of activity, which is exactly what I did right after I left my corporate job. I later discovered there's a lot of value in sitting quietly. You need to allow yourself a break so you can make better choices.
- **Mother yourself a little.** When familiar routines suddenly dissolve, it can seem as if all your supports are gone. For a while after I lost my job, I had the sense that I was in a free

fall. It's crucial, while absorbing the shock of the new, to make yourself feel pampered.

- **Ignore your inner reptile.** The part of the human mind that is often referred to as the "lizard brain" existed in even the earliest land animals. The lizard brain is concerned with survival, and it's likely to pipe up with warning sirens during times of change. But in the modern world, it's like a misfiring car alarm: pointless and annoying.

- **Silence your inner know-it-all.** If you're so smart that you can't rethink your position, all your IQ points won't do you much good when your life is turned upside down. Go inward and seek a new path.

- **Seek new perspectives.** Zen practitioners cultivate the "don't know" mind; they work to assume they don't know anything and see the world with fresh eyes. This is a great way to approach change: as an opportunity to start anew, to consider all possibilities.

- **Try something new and slightly scary.** Why? Because now is the time to explore what it is that you really like. Catch yourself off guard and see what happens.

- **Be skeptical of common wisdom.** It is OK to experience the moment and enjoy all the gifts it brings, but you also need to figure out your next move. One year, everyone thinks you need an MBA to succeed at anything. The next, they're saying that there are no jobs out there anyway, so don't even try. Don't listen! Set your sights on what you think is important, and you will achieve success.

- **Learn to live with uncertainty.** You'll feel more confident and alive each time you push past your boundaries.

- **Shed the old you.** When you start to turn this sudden shift in your life to your advantage, you might shake up a lot of people, especially the ones who aren't happy with how they're living. To them, your efforts to move forward may feel like a glaring searchlight that needs to be quickly switched off. Discard physical clutter, tired ideas, and old routines. Seeing things through another's fresh eyes can help.

"As iron sharpens iron, so a friend sharpens a friend."
—*Proverbs 27:17* NLT

Let's celebrate together!

4

Family, Friends, and Relationships

"The best and most beautiful things in the world cannot be seen or even touched. They must be felt with the heart."
—Helen Keller

When you make any kind of change, it's going to be easier with support, but you don't always have the right people at the right time. Start by cleaning house of users, abusers, and other toxic people who are draining your time and energy. Invite people into your life who are loving, helpful, energizing, and supportive.

Sherri Elliott-Yeary

Many Christian couples I know consistently cite an inability to communicate as one of their biggest problems. But the communication issue is not confined to challenges in marriage; it is also a key factor in nearly every relationship I can think of.

Understanding differences in personalities, as well as placing value in differences and making a decision to honor and respect others, will greatly improve your communication and thus your relationships.

Some of us like to believe other people around us are perfect, that they've chosen just the right support network of people who can make their lives easier. A support network can consist of friends, a spouse, family, and mentors. You may not get to pick your family, but at least you can pick your friends and your mentors. Take advantage by picking healthy friends and mentors and avoiding toxic relationships. People come and go; they change for better or worse. You are not obligated to keep toxic people in your life just because you have a history with them.

I am constantly challenging myself to stretch my inner circle to include new friends, but I recognize that I am not personally responsible for them, nor do I need to invest in them as much as others. I have a choice.

I am often asked, "Who's your mentor?" I can't pin it down to one person. I've been blessed by many mentors in different ways and at different times. One person can mentor you on starting a business, another on balancing family and career. If you model or collaborate with only one person you'll always be one step behind him or her, but if you model many, you can lead the pack. Choose the mentors in your life because they have something interesting to say and an interesting way of saying it. Learn from their mistakes as well as their successes. Think of your mentors as a collective genius with which you can bounce ideas around and perfect your vision. Magnify your intelligence through theirs.

I'm blessed by so many great relationships. My girlfriends have inspired me to be a better mother, wife, friend, and caring professional.

As I have grown more mature, I've learned the valuable lesson that it is OK to rely on the right girlfriends. I've also learned to eliminate the "takers" from my life so I can enjoy relationships with "givers," the women on whom I know I can depend and trust. My girlfriends and I may not connect for months, but if any of them truly needed me, I would be there for them in any capacity, as they are there for me. Women connect with each other differently and provide support systems that help each other to deal with stress and difficult life experiences. Physically, this quality "girlfriend time" helps us to create more serotonin, a neurotransmitter that helps combat depression and can create a general feeling of well-being. Women share feelings whereas men often form relationships around activities, like golf. They rarely sit down with a buddy and talk about how they feel about certain things or how their personal lives are going. Jobs? Yes. Sports? Yes. But their feelings? Rarely.

A friend of mine just took an evening class at Stanford and shared some of her professor's insights with me. One of his lectures was on the mind–body connection and the relationship between stress and disease. The professor, who is also head of the psychiatry department at Stanford, said that one of the best things a man could do for his health is to be married to a woman, whereas for a woman, one of the best things she could do for her health was to nurture her relationships with her girlfriends. Many of the class attendees laughed, but the professor was serious.

There's a tendency to think that when we are exercising we are doing something good for our bodies, but when we are hanging out with friends we are wasting our time and should be more productively engaged. That's not true! The professor said spending time with a friend is just as important to our general health as jogging or working out at a gym.

To support what women already knew, a new study from researchers in Utah found that good social relationships encourage a healthy lifespan, and that maintaining these relationships may be as important to your lifespan as quitting smoking or losing weight. The analysis, which was compiled from 148 other relevant studies covering over 308,000 people, found that people with strong social relationships were 50 percent less likely to die early than those without similar support.

In fact, researchers likened poor social relationships to smoking up to fifteen cigarettes a day or being an alcoholic. Poor social relationships were also found to be *more* harmful than not exercising and twice as harmful as obesity.

The study also found that Americans are becoming more isolated, with three times as many Americans reporting "having no confidant" than those surveyed twenty years ago. And since loneliness is contagious, this isolation could be the start of future health problems. The researchers concluded that we need to start viewing our social relationships as an important part of our overall health. Spending more time with my girlfriends will help me live longer? Sign me up!

So every time you hang out to schmooze with your girlfriends, pat yourself on the back and congratulate yourself for doing something good for your health and spirit. We are indeed very lucky to have each other. I feel like my circle of friends just keeps growing, and my heart grows bigger with each person who touches my life.

Helene Terry
Award-Winning Kitchen and Bath Designer

In my work many of my clients are friends, so it may appear that I am not working very hard when we are at lunch laughing and talking, yet I am actually building strong relationships with past, present, and future clients.

I believe you must love your profession in order to do this. I read design magazines and tour special homes on my own during my "off" time, so am I still working or am I playing? When the lines between work, friends, and fulfillment are blurred, that's a good thing.

In the business world, I align myself with other successful women through networking and constantly seek ways of learning more about my profession. Through volunteering, I learn more about my other personal interests while serving others at the same time. Multitasking on every level works well for me.

I've learned to use other professionals to round out the areas where I am not as strong. We cannot be experts in all areas, so learning my weaknesses has also been my strength. I stay in my area of specialization and become a great complement with others' gifts and talents, professionally as well as personally. Everyone wins with this approach.

When I divorced, my ex-husband relinquished all rights to my daughter. It made me realize it was up to me to provide total support for us, so I took my job very seriously. I knew we needed support, so I moved closer to his family, which was in the same metropolitan area, so that they could enjoy a relationship with her.

It was imperative for me to find a way to forgive him so that I would not stay stuck in anger and resentment. That healing only came about with therapy from a Christian-based psychiatrist. I am convinced that the therapy greatly contributed to the wonderful, positive attitude that my daughter and I now possess.

God has kept a protective hand on the two of us and helped me find forgiveness and relinquish the anger, keeping our home and attitudes positive. It has not been an easy road; yet by keeping my focus on the prize—raising a well-adjusted and loving daughter—I was able to get help along the way during these difficult times to reach this goal.

I was in a wonderful, coed, single parent Sunday school class when my daughter was younger. We formed our own babysitting co-op, helped each other with home chores, and became each other's family.

I'm still in touch with several of these friends, though many of us have married or moved away.

You cannot do it alone. Friends, faith, and family are incredibly important to your success. Even if you are able to get to the top by yourself, what fun is it to have a glass of champagne alone? The old adage about having strength in numbers has been true for me.

Kimberly Davis
Leadership Trainer

My life and career seem to be in constant evolution, as *balance* isn't something that comes naturally for me. I've always tended to be a give-everything-150 percent type of gal, and it's impossible to give that on all fronts. The only constant in my life is the process of evaluation.

I evaluate my husband's needs, my son's needs, my needs, the business's needs, and the needs of my friends. I'm hyper-aware that they all take the investment of time and energy, and I *feel* it when I've not invested. There's a price I pay inside.

My strategy is to show compassion to myself and to listen deeply to those around me for what's *really* needed. I take time to check in with my heart and remember to breathe. I surround myself with other incredible women who share a hunger for rich relationships, self-actualization, and the need to make a difference—women who inspire me to seek balance in life, no matter how elusive. I try to look for what's right and be grateful.

I think my wiring definitely came from my parents. My dad was (and still is) a big-time workaholic, always driving toward something and unable to be really present with the people right in front of him. He's an amazing and brilliant man with a huge heart. But I suspect he doesn't really believe that about himself, and is still in some way trying to prove that he's OK.

I know from experience the price he's paid for focusing primarily on his work; he's missed out on a lot, and I could have gone down that path too.

My mom is a beautiful, creative spirit who put herself on the back-burner for her family, and also paid a price. I saw her struggle with self-confidence and a sense of powerlessness, and

I felt her dissatisfaction as she put her dreams aside. I could have gone down that path as well.

But I think *my path* was forged not just from what I learned from my parents, but from what I learned from my brother. In 1987 my brother Todd was in a head-on collision that changed everything for our family. Todd survived, with a great deal of trauma, and has spent the past twenty years battling for normalcy and trying to find his place in the world. He is the wisest, most soulful person I know.

In an instant, life as we knew it was shattered. What once was so important now seemed pointless. New perspectives emerged from the wreckage. Life seemed more fragile and precious.

From Todd's accident, I learned that however I spent my time, it needed to be purposeful. I wanted to make an impact. When I felt I wasn't able to make an impact, I grew restless, no longer content just to have a job.

From Todd's accident, I learned that my relationships are more important than anything else. Do I need to make amends? Does this person know I *care*? Do they feel *seen*? Do the people I love *experience being loved*?

I learned that I may not get another shot, so I better play all out. When I find myself holding back, I feel it big-time. I'm so aware of how easily it can all change that my inner compass starts sending out an alarm to "Take action!" when I start allowing myself to play small.

But maybe more than anything, I've recalibrated for myself what "playing all out" looks like. I realize my job is to bring the best me into the world that I can, which doesn't mean attaining success at the expense of my family, or catering solely to the needs of my family at the expense of reaching my potential. It's about trying to integrate all of it, the "balance" that we're talking about.

I'm always looking for new ways to learn. If I were to give advice, I think I'd say, "Be kind to yourself." No one is perfect. It's an illusion. Give yourself the latitude to mess up and then to powerfully choose a new course. Make it right for yourself and others. Make it right for your business. Make it right for your family. Make it right for your friends. Just make it right.

Balance is worth seeking. It's elusive as hell. But it's in the *journey toward balance* that the magic lives. It's worth taking the journey.

Dea Richard

Director for a National Staffing Firm

I lost my husband seven years ago in a motorcycle accident, and I am raising two teenage boys on my own. They were ages nine and eleven when their dad died. I was a corporate trainer in sales and computers and traveled a lot. Their father was a stay-at-home dad, so I got grounded overnight.

My employers understood. They gave me a lot of space and allowed me to work from home, but it was still too much. I downgraded myself, working thirty hours when I used to put in fifty hours a week.

I'm independent, and it's hard for me to ask for help. This experience was a big eye-opener for me: it's OK to ask for help and admit I can't do it all myself.

My "village" really pitched in. My husband's nephew, who was in his early twenties, moved in with us to help with child care and support. As a follower of martial arts, he displayed courage, poise, and respect to my young boys and he was never too tired to play video games with them. One of my brothers moved his family a half mile down the road from us so they could be close enough to lend a hand when we needed. One of our biggest sources of support has been my children's grandparents. In spite of their own grief, they have always been there whenever we needed them. My neighbors would come by and offer to help; when my fence blew down, they came and helped me put it back up. That's my idea of a village.

My boys and I went to grief counseling, and the counselor gave me guidelines. "Don't change too many things right now," was one. And "Give the boys a sense of normalcy," was another.

It changed my relationship with my sons quite a bit. My oldest son sought out other male role models. My husband used to take all the kids fishing, so when he died, the neighborhood dads stepped up and took my sons camping and hunting. Other neighborhood dads were proactive because they knew my boys needed to be around and learn from other men.

I really made it because of family and friends. When you experience a loss, don't expect to be able to do it all. As women, we think we have to do it all. You have to ask for help; you will be stronger for it. When you deny others the opportunity to help, you are not only denying yourself, you are also denying them the joy that comes from helping.

Donna Bender

Founder of a Marketing and Strategy Firm

I am still on my journey "to have it all." The key is appreciating what you have at the time. I believe that our greatest challenges and obstacles can be, at times, ourselves. Having friends to call when you are down—when you are not sure where you will get the strength to get out of bed, take care of a child, or move forward—makes all the difference in the world.

On my thirtieth birthday, I thought I had it all. I was vice president of two major apparel companies and making $100,000 a year. Yet there was something missing in my life. I'd been married for twelve years. I was burned out, traveling too much, and I wanted to be a mother so badly. By this point, I was at a high-risk age to get pregnant, but you know the famous saying, "Man plans and God laughs."

Well, my beautiful daughter was born and we had an immediate connection. I know that mothers can understand what I mean. My daughter and I locked eyes, and that was it!

I felt that I needed to come up with a solution that would generate income for my family and also allow me to stay child-focused. So I came up with an idea to fix the situation: I created a company where my husband could have a position and I could continue to center my interests on children.

Through hard work and not allowing those negative voices to deter me, we formed a company with business partners and our children's clothing line was sold to specialty stores and department stores around the country.

Everything seemed great until my partners asked me to fire my husband, which resulted in me losing the company. With the emotional support of good friends and by having a strong, spiritual personality, I was able to rebuild my life by teaching wellness for the next five years; this was probably one of the happiest and healthiest times of my life.

By the time my daughter reached high school, there were too many kids applying for the neighborhood high school. She was accepted to a school forty minutes away from our home. I knew this was a sign to move away from New York, so I hired an educational consultant and, after much consideration, we chose Dallas.

I did not know one person when I moved to Dallas in 2005, but I couldn't have picked a better city. My daughter turned to me after two months of living here and said she wished she had lived here her whole life. The people are some of the friendliest people I have ever met; they are so eager to take you under their wings and introduce you to others.

After all of the dust settled and my daughter was well-situated in school, with great determination and what I now call "The Art of Networking," I started my current business, helping others brand themselves and build their image. I have reinvented myself many times. If I can help others overcome uncertainty about their business and brand by supporting them, I have accomplished my goal. This is a reminder to many of us: our own inner strength and wisdom are our compass, even when we may not be able to feel it.

When we are frozen in our own tracks and don't know where to turn, there is definitely hope and people out there to help and support us.

I don't believe I have met one woman (except perhaps a doctor or lawyer) who is in her current occupation because she planned it that way. I do know, however, that strength, perseverance, and determination are important rules to live by to overcome whatever hand is dealt you. I think it is my inherent drive that keeps me going, along with my friends, family, and partners who have been the wind beneath my wings.

Sherri's Tips:
Create Healthy Relationships

- **Choose friends wisely.** You do not have to be everyone's friend. Choose to be friends with people who build you up, not tear you down.
- **Listen.** Listen closely to what the other person is saying. Let that person know you truly hear them by actively listening and giving them your full and undivided attention. Summarize what you've heard.
- **Avoid mothering your friends.** By all means, if a friend asks for your advice, give it. Perhaps life is throwing them a curve ball when they need your support or insight. Don't wiggle your way into every aspect of your friend's life, telling them how to be the star of their own show. Give them room to process things and make their own decisions.
- **Be authentic.** Be yourself. Be honest. Avoid putting up a façade. If someone can't accept you for who you are, developing a relationship with that person will be hard. Don't shortchange yourself by denying your beliefs, values, and point of view for the sake of fitting in. You won't be doing yourself any favors.
- **Respect their choices.** If your friend decides to make a move when you think standing still is the right thing to do, let that friend do her thing. If you've given your advice and your friend sees things differently, step aside. She might be making a mistake, but if it doesn't kill her, she can learn from

the experience. And if it will kill her, lock her in a closet and don't let her out until she has forgotten why you trapped her in there in the first place.

- **Be the kind of friend you want others to be for you.** You want friends who are honest, kind, compassionate, fair, non-judgmental, authentic, and intelligent. Be that person first, and you'll be more likely to attract that kind of friend into your life.

- **Express your gratitude.** Let your friends know you value their friendship. Tell them. Write them a note. Surprise a friend by taking her out for lunch or dinner at one of her favorite places. These things say, "You're important to me."

- **Admit and apologize.** When you do something wrong, admit it. Learn to apologize. Sometimes a friend is upset, and all she wants from you is for you to take ownership of your misstep and apologize.

- **Keep your promises.** If you make a promise, do your best to keep it.

- **Friendships grow, change, and sometimes end.** The person you were when you met someone is not who you will always be. Sometimes we struggle to hang on to a wilting relationship. Many times, it is healthier to let go.

"There is no greater love than to lay down one's life for one's friends"
—John 15:13 NLT

5

Men,
Women, and
the Workplace

"Men are allies in the women's revolution, because it's
good for families, and good for business."
—Nancy Clark

*Men and women communicate and make decisions differently, but there's
no question that the two management styles can be compatible if given the
chance. With women constituting 50 percent of the workforce and making
85 percent of consumer buying decisions, maybe it's time we paid attention
to boosting the number of women on sales teams, on executive boards, and
in all areas of business.*

Sherri Elliott-Yeary

I believe that men and women can actually become one through
understanding, value, and honor. We all need each other, and
even when we don't agree on everything, we can learn to disagree

while still showing respect for each other's differences. Men have as much right to an opinion as we do.

Ninety-three percent of communication is said to be nonverbal. Sixty-eight percent is the tone of your voice; facial expression or body language account for the remaining difference.

As women relating to our mates, our male supervisors, and other men with whom we work, we need to be aware that men normally respond out of logic and women tend to respond more out of emotion. This does not make one right and the other wrong, but understanding the differences helps.

I remember my first networking event like it was yesterday. It was a local Chamber of Commerce meet and greet; as I walked into the room, a cold sweat came over me. I marched myself into the ladies room, got on my knees, and prayed to God for the strength and wisdom to network and share with these people and not make a fool of myself.

I walked back into the meeting room, and, with a keen eye, spotted a table that was almost full, but seated there were only men and no other women. I knew, based on my corporate experience, that men are typically the decision makers in business, so I chose to sit with them.

When I started my consulting company, I hadn't realized that I'd never sold as part of what I call a *job*. This is a dilemma many women face as they leave behind the trappings of a *job*, like healthcare benefits, paid vacation, etc., for the ability to work for themselves when and how they want. I jokingly state that the only way I would leave the cushy, flexible schedule I have that meets my family and work balance is for great medical benefits.

As a then-single-mother starting my own business in an effort to establish myself in the consulting world, I had to find the tools and abilities to successfully sell my services to prospective clients.

After I took my seat, I noticed a beautiful and elegant blonde lady getting up from her table to come to my table and sit down next to me. After the networking event, she introduced herself as JoAnna Couch, the Corporate Educator. During our conversation she asked, "What made you choose this table?" I replied, "God provided me the answer to my prayer and I took the seat that I was directed to, at a table with all men."

All I did was take my place among men as an equal, but I didn't realize I was making a bold sociological statement and setting an example for other women to follow.

Later, as I got to know JoAnna, she revealed that she had watched me enter the room, analyze the tables, then take a seat at the only all-male table in the room. We talked about the fear I had to overcome and the faith I called upon to do it. She became my coach and mentor during the first few years of my business, and now I am honored to call her my friend as well.

Since then, business has changed and I've changed along with it, consulting my clients to be aware of sociological shifts that may affect their business. In fact, that's my specialty: generational differences, gender differences, team-building, and other human behaviors related to the new workforce.

According to the latest Deloitte study, *Human Capital Trends 2011,* the corporate ladder has been replaced by the corporate lattice—a mathematically based design that extends the workforce structure in many directions, not just up and down. Work is no longer a place where rewards are tied to climbing the corporate ladder. Instead, the lattice matrix is virtual, project-based, gender-inclusive, multicultural, multigenerational, and team-leader oriented.

This new structure allows many avenues for corporations to develop talent and for individuals to build careers, and that's why it represents a fundamental change in the American workforce. No longer is a woman defined by a title; she's defined by what she can do. Boundaries no longer matter: an employee or contractor can work from home or log in from across the ocean. Their contributions are task-oriented and quantifiable, making whip-hands (middle-managers) less relevant, too.

While the lattice concept was introduced by Deloitte, the consulting company found that it extends all the way to executive levels. In the executive lattice, leadership is also collective, which is ideal for women since we are natural collaborators.

What's driving the trend, says the report, are fewer levels of management, the demise of the single-income nuclear family, virtual workplaces, and, believe it or not, the changing needs of men who "cite more work–life conflict than women do."

Not only are women half of the US workforce, they hold 60 percent of undergraduate and master's degrees. Forty percent of women are the primary breadwinners for their families. More than 80 percent of consumer purchases in the developed world are made by women, according to Deutsche Bank Research in 2010.

The traditional one-rung-at-a-time career path doesn't work for women because we are also primary caregivers, often raising children and helping aging parents all at the same time. Many of us drop out of the workforce to have children and stay out until we are content that they can be well cared for by others.

After struggling to have it all, women are abandoning or not even trying to get C-level jobs, eradicating many of the cultural gains the women's movement of the twentieth century worked so hard to achieve. It comes as no surprise that older workers want a better life–work balance, similar to what the millennial generation states they require.

Why are women in only 11 percent of American corporate C-level jobs? Are men scared of the diminishing upper management jobs, protecting their own, or are women simply abandoning a system that doesn't work for either sex any longer? Whatever the cause, women are leaving corporate America to pursue their own passions. One thing is certain: gender balance in leadership and the workplace only works if both genders are allowed to be who they are. For example, women tend to take fewer investment risks, base more of their economic decisions on the welfare of their families, and save more than men, according to research from Goldman Sachs.

It's a business issue, not a women's issue. If Deloitte is right, the issues of flexibility, autonomy, mobility, and even child care increasingly affect both genders. That means women can't abandon the boardroom. We have the numbers and the education. We can climb the corporate lattice and make it work for us in a way that the corporate ladder never did.

Men understand return on investment (ROI). Women understand the value of return on relationships (ROR). Now's the time to make your mark!

Judy Hoberman
Author and Speaker
Specializing in Gender Communication

In sales, men are transactional. They like to close the deal and then build a relationship. Women like to build a relationship first, then close the deal.

I've been in sales for thirty years, always in male-dominated industries. Because I was the one of a few females in sales, I had to figure out a way to be successful using my own methods. I started with no knowledge of insurance, but I quickly became a top producer in the company and was promoted through the ranks to become one of the top agency managers. In this new role, I did the recruiting and the training. I then became a corporate employee for the company and was transferred to Texas. I built a sales training program, and an internal university, then I resigned. I wanted to go back to being an entrepreneur. I knew if I didn't, I was going to disappear. I decided to build my company and that's when the next chapter of my life began.

My passion is building businesses from scratch, which is what I did with Selling In A Skirt. I wanted to help women in sales who had no female mentors. I thought about what I had needed when coming up through the ranks and brought that to the table. Here is an example: A young woman called me looking for some help in sales training. Her boss told her she needed to be more aggressive and close the deal the first time out. We talked about the benefit of building a relationship rather than being transactional and grabbing a check.

I put together a proposal for her to receive coaching and asked her to read it all the way to the end. What I wrote at the very bottom was, "You are me thirty years ago. If I had someone that would have stepped up to the plate and mentored me, things would have been so different." I offered to be her mentor going forward.

As a female working in a male-dominated industry, many times you have to work harder just to gain credibility. Many times you aren't even really wanted. Sometimes there might be a quota to fill or points the company may receive because you are a woman. The best-case scenario is that you are wanted and needed in the position, and even then you have to prove that you are intelligent.

What I do in my programs is all based on relationships, a trait innate with women. Many successful men are realizing that in order to be successful, this is something that both genders need to be proficient at and understand.

How do you start a relationship? One way is to ask open-ended questions; for example, what are the client's challenges, what are they looking for, and what is important to them? It's a dialog between the client and the salesperson or manager. If you ask the right questions, you will get to the close naturally. After all my other questions, I always ask, "Is there anything else?" If the customer or client says yes, I continue asking questions. If they tell me that there isn't anything else, the result is a natural close. Instead of going out saying, "I have to get the check," tell yourself, "I'm going to start a relationship and the check is the by-product of the relationship."

When I was actively selling, my goal was to make everyone my friend and have everyone think of me as their trusted advisor. After a short amount of time, I worked strictly on referrals. Everyone in my office wanted to know how I did it. Even though my sales calls took longer, I closed more business because I built relationships with my clients. Building relationships takes time, but it's worth the investment.

When I train men on how to communicate with women, I advise them that women want to be treated equally, not identically. Men and women have differences—neither is right or wrong—and if we made our differences assets and not liabilities, just think how much more powerful your sales team could be. I don't bash men or cajole women. We do things differently, but when we understand the differences and embrace them, the bottom line will go up.

Men are typically more transactional; they think in bullet points. They want the beginning and the end and don't care about the middle. If they want to know the middle of the story, they will ask for it. Women want to be painted into the picture. They want to know how your product or service will affect them and everyone around them.

Here is an example of painting someone into the picture. I always confirmed appointments, and I'd ask for directions off the highway. I would always repeat the directions back with one part reversed. This way they were listening and started to see me coming to their house. They would wait for me to make sure I didn't get lost. This was before cell phones. When I arrived, they were excited because I was now part of their life.

My relationship with my clients would begin on the phone. The men in my office would sell on the phone with the mindset of picking up a check. I sold the appointment. I would do my fact finding, so when I arrived there I had the solution they needed. It's all about building relationships, and if you can do that, you'll be successful. The world is not a transactional place any longer. In order to be successful in today's economy, whether you are male or female, you have to be relational.

Because women are responsible for purchasing 85 percent of consumer products, and they are now 50 percent of the US workforce, you need both men and women on your team.

Depending on the situation, you need to have people that are transactional as well as relational. There are situations for both styles. Case in point, if I am in a rush, I would prefer to get right to the point and expect the bullet points. If you use the right approach at the right time, your client will give you the cues if you are paying attention.

Men look for facts and figures and features and benefits, and they are more accustomed to using closed-ended questions to get the information. Women, looking to start a conversation, will use open-ended questions to accomplish this.

My appointments may have taken longer, but I built long-term relationships with my clients. Women look for long-term relationships. When they find someone they trust, they will be your biggest source of referrals. And isn't that what it's all about?

Jackie Agers
Licensed, Professional Counselor
Specializing in Family Therapy and Addiction

There is a Chinese quote that I use in therapy, "We don't change by trying to change; we change by figuring out what keeps us the same." Awareness is the real cure; I learned that from my mentor. This helps out-of-balance single moms, who strive to gain more ownership of their children, reset priorities and have more valuable time with them. Children remember love and safety, not starched shirts and clean bathrooms.

One reason we keep ourselves from experiencing happiness is we think happiness is a destination with a neon sign at the end of a road. That's Cinderella thinking. Happiness is really how we feel along the journey.

One area of focus for me is helping my clients live in the moment. You can live now; you can't live in the past or future—you must be in the here and now.

I work with young women to assist them in looking at their blessings rather than focusing on what they don't have. Focusing on what they don't have is negative energy and can ruin their day and their lives.

I see a trend of middle-aged women going back to college and putting pressure on themselves to compete against others with their looks, their achievements, and their goals. Yet they still feel like they fall short. Our own culture produces this falsehood. These women didn't come into the world comparing themselves; they learned that from listening to other people's opinions.

So how do we prevent our culture from forcing us to compete and rate ourselves against each other? We have to learn where we stop and the world begins. I give my clients tools to assist them to take responsibility for their own actions and not take responsibility for others. I teach them to have personal boundaries, because if they let other people take bites out of them, they feel hurt and empty. That's the concept of a boundary.

Dr. Sue Hummel
Professor of Dentistry

How did I balance my time between family, finances, friends, and fulfillment? Woody Allen said 90 percent of success is showing up. Although he's not my idol, I do think that statement is true.

Very few can have it all. If you have to work for a living, you're going reach a certain level of success and, unless you are willing to give up family, you probably cannot have it all. The thing is to be happy with where you land.

I would rather have my job where I am needed, and the freedom to be there for my family when they need me, than to be higher up in the administration, where I have to be there all the time.

Being a single parent, I had to limit my career to be at my daughter's school events and extracurricular activities. I was asked to do a lot of things outside of work, such as speaking engagements, but by the time I did the math (babysitters, time, etc.) it just didn't make sense. I would tell my bosses that I had responsibilities at home, it would cost me X amount of dollars, and I could not justify spending my money that way. A lot of people (i.e., men) did not like this, but they didn't have to do the work or spend the money, so my conscience was at peace.

My parents have Alzheimer's and Parkinson's and my sister was diagnosed with terminal cancer. I took a formal leave of absence to spend time with them. Fortunately I was not one of those people that abused sick time or vacation time, so I was able to schedule paid time to be with them for two weeks at a time every three to four months, since I live sixteen hours from them.

My boss was supportive because I was able to schedule my time off at less crucial times. He did contact me almost every day by e-mail when I was gone, and I was able to give him solutions and answers to his questions, so my being gone was not a burden to him.

I run a clinic, but I could do a bigger job. I don't want a bigger job because I would lose the part of my job I like the most, which is student–patient contact and solving problems. The higher up you go, you may have to deal with administrative problems, and that's really not fun to me. I know some people like that type of thing, and I'm thankful they are alive and doing it, but I realized about ten years ago that I wanted to be closer to what was happening between students and patients.

I would hate not to spend any time with my family because I had a "big" job. To me, it wouldn't be worth it. But some people don't have those attachments because of the way they grew up or they simply don't want to be there.

It's a personal choice, and I'm happy with the choices I've made.

Sherri's Tips:
Better Communication Between Men and Women in the Workplace

Typical Complaints Women Have about Men:
- Addressing women as "girl," "gal," "honey," "hon," "baby girl," "lady," or "darlin'"
- Making women into objects: "I have a car, a boat, a dog, and a wife."
- Using expressions that reference violence or sexual connotations: "We murdered (screwed, stuck it to, etc.) the competition."
- Making decisions about work with each other and not including women, then telling the women, "Last night we got together and decided . . ."

Typical Complaints Men Have about Women:
- Not getting down to business soon enough
- Taking things too seriously or being too sensitive
- Trying to be "one of the boys" (using profanity, telling sexist jokes, etc.)

Gender Communication Tip Sheet

WOMEN	MEN
Share experiences to show commonality	Focus on statistics, rankings
Build off of each other's discussion points	Relate by sharing stories to "one up" each other

Strategy: Women need to get to the bottom line quickly and succinctly. Men need to understand that when a woman tells a story, she is building common ground with you.

Want to talk about the problem and solve it collaboratively	Move to solutions and problem-solving right away
Emphasize feelings and communication	Place high value on ability to achieve results
Process as a way to include others and build relationships	Prefer activity over discussion

Strategy: Women, don't try to get men to talk if they're not ready. Observe and listen rather than process out loud. Men, understand that processing is a way for women to include others and build relationships.

Offer help and advice as a sign of caring	Don't ask for help; believe it makes them weaker

Strategy: Women, understand that offering help may be interpreted as a lack of trust in another's ability. Don't be so quick to offer advice. Men, ask what you can do to help. It may be an opportunity to show support and caring.

Strengths Associated with Women at Work
- Harmony, balance, nurturance, serenity, creativity, and vision
- Teamwork and collaboration
- Long-term problem solving; greater good–oriented

Strengths Associated with Men at Work
- Goal-oriented
- Tangible accomplishments
- Immediate problem solving
- Singleness of purpose

"May God, who gives this patience and encouragement,
help you live in complete harmony with each other, as is fitting
for followers of Christ Jesus"
—*Romans 15:5* NLT

6

Money,
Money,
Money

"A big part of financial freedom is having your heart and mind
free from worry about the what-ifs of life."
—Suzie Orman

*What's your relationship with money? If you're like most of us, due to
the downturn in the economy you have a new respect for money—not only
for what it can buy, but how it can insulate you from fear. The pursuit of
money is as important to women as having families. Women are marrying
and having children later in life in order to pursue their careers. Then a
funny thing happens on the way to the boardroom . . . women are burned
out and dropping out, deciding to open their own businesses, so they can
work at their own pace.*

Sherri Elliott-Yeary

The best way I have found to determine if God is first in my life is to slow down and ask myself some simple questions: What do I think about the most? What is the first thing on my mind in the morning and the last thing on my mind at night? What do I pray for and talk about the most? What subjects fill my conversations with God and with others? What do I do with my time?

Let me ask you some questions: What about your money? Is it easy for you to spend money on a new outfit complete with new jewelry and shoes or something for the house, but difficult to obey God at offering time or support the homeless in your community? Do you find it easier to spend money on eating out than on Christian teachings or buying food for the local food bank?

Money in itself is not evil: it's the love of money that can be the root of all evil. If you love God and your community more than you love money, you can do with your money what God tells you to and be at peace. I challenge you to regularly stop and take a good look at your life. Ask for guidance to see where your priorities are out of line. Then adjust your lifestyle choices to gain peace around the choices you make daily with regard to your finances. This is a habit I rely on every time I am remotely close to a shoe store!

My mom was a single parent who raised four children alone, and I was the eldest. I learned at a very young age two important lessons: have a financial plan in case of an emergency, and never depend on your spouse to be the only breadwinner.

My dad divorced my mom when I was ten years old, and he and his girlfriend moved three thousand miles away. My mom had to raise four kids with no support, and it was not easy for her. Growing up as a kid on welfare taught me the importance of working hard to support myself and never allowing someone else the power to take away my home or my livelihood.

Ignorance is not bliss when it comes to your money—I know! When I started my career in human resources, my daughter was two years old, and I was a single parent with no child support. Now, as a happily married woman, I've prayed for God to show me the path of trust to allow my husband to be not only my life partner, but also my partner in all financial matters related to my business and our personal life.

Although most of us know that money does not buy happiness, the lack of money can bring plenty of hardship. If you are living your life without financial peace or reserves, it's impossible to be in control of your life. When we have to live paycheck to paycheck, or work in a *job* that drains our soul, we end up feeling empty and afraid—not filled with hope and passion.

Many books have been written about money; they range from "how to make smart investments" to "how to be debt-free in thirty days." But I've yet to see a book that combines basic money management skills with the more emotional and spiritual changes necessary to create a healthy, prosperous *relationship* with money.

Can you afford to live the life you really want? I don't mean "keeping up with the Joneses" by driving a fancy car or living in a big home. That's about quantity. I'm talking about having the freedom to make decisions that give you the *quality* of life you desire. That's why it's important for you to become the CEO of your career, life, and finances. Women understand enterprise. Whether you choose to start a venture of your own, manage your family, or build a corporate career, enterprise is already inside you. Just tap into it!

While women are enterprising, not every woman is entrepreneurial. Only you know which path of success fits your personality and passionate vision. As the CEO of your life, you must also be the CEO of your career. I am known to jokingly share this nugget when speaking, "I am the CEO of my consulting practice, which means I am the Chief Everything Officer."

You must be able to choose if you are more the corporate kind of girl or the rebel who wants to be an entrepreneur. There is a thrill of sorts when you "eat what you kill," but it's not for every woman.

I chose to be an entrepreneur when I launched my first business over eight years ago. I did not research the gaps in the industry to match my passionate vision and aptitude like I should have, but I knew in my heart that I was ready to risk it all to support my vision of what I wanted my life to be. I knew my value proposition was to educate leaders on the critical reasons to develop the people in the workplace.

For some the path I took would work, but others may need to conduct market research and hone in on the exact service they want to provide before they take the entrepreneurial leap. For others, it would be more attractive to take a corporate role. Trust me, I have had moments when a corporate role seems attractive when I am working all hours of the night to get a speech finished before a big event.

For me, it's all about listening to my inner voice and learning to trust my instincts. This is how I started a business, bought a business, authored my first book, and became an international speaker. This path has afforded me the financial ability to live life fully and passionately on my terms with balance.

Just as we need to be clear on what makes us happy, we also need to be honest about what it means to be wealthy. Far too often the word "wealth" relates to money, social status, and possessions—perpetuated by the media and amplified by celebrity gossip. I want you to try to see wealth not as a tally of valuable assets or stock portfolio but rather as a barometer of inner peace and contentment. Given this definition, "wealthy" means you are healthy, happy, and safe.

We all have done it. We see something we like, we feel we gotta-have-it, we rush, and we buy it. No questions asked—until now.

Once you are aware of the vision of the life you want, the see–want–buy process is going to stop. You will no longer (I mean it: you really will no longer) go from see to want to buy in an instant. You will see something, want it, but then pause to ask yourself, "Will this thing (or action or word or decision) move me closer to the vision I have for the life I want?" If the answer is yes, then if you can afford it you may give yourself permission to go ahead and buy that particular item.

If you're ready to enjoy your life, have balance, and gain financial health, you have two areas to explore:

The Inner Work: Change How You Think and Feel About Money

1. Change your beliefs.
2. Develop an attitude of gratitude.
3. Share your wealth.
4. Get comfortable with more.
5. Respect yourself.

The Outer Work: Develop New Money Skills

1. Ask for help.
2. Balance your accounts or outsource it.
3. Know where your money goes.
4. Cut your expenses.
5. Pay your bills on time.
6. Eliminate debt.

Jean M. Danner

Human Resources Executive

Why are some people so distraught about change? If you're prepared financially and professionally, there's nothing to fear.

I have worked for a company that was acquired and for a company that acquired other businesses, divested units of its own, and even experienced a hostile takeover attempt (a deal which eventually fell through). In human resources, when this type of activity occurs, you're in the middle of it. We watch people go through it, and it is interesting how many respond with fear, panic, or denial. Most people are afraid because they don't prepare for changes.

I have always made sure I had choices. It's all about showing people other options and learning that you don't have to do everything the conventional way.

Women are often unprepared. In the financial services company where I worked, all the senior executives were men. Many had been with the company for a long time, and their wives handled the majority of their personal obligations, i.e., housework, family obligations, child care issues, etc. I didn't have that option; I had to make sure I was better prepared so I could stand on my own in the event of a crisis and not fall back or make excuses. I made sure I had great child care and back-up support to step in when needed.

I would work with women and tell them, "If you want to be successful, you need contingency plans. You certainly can't take care of your family if you're unemployed. You have to protect your income. Things happen; life is messy, so be prepared."

As a single parent, I made sure I could take care of myself and my daughter. I put my raises into savings and didn't spend my money foolishly. I kept my education fresh. I'm not saying everyone has to get a master's degree, but if you're in a career where having that degree is a competitive advantage, then you need to get one.

I would recommend you go to seminars and conferences and keep yourself current with the changes and advances in your chosen industry. If I ever did get laid off, I know I'd be OK, because I'm financially and professionally prepared.

If you have the skills and will to succeed, you'll come across as confident, and that will go a long way.

Here are my top five suggestions for avoiding and recovering from job loss:

- Practice personal accountability.
- Don't wonder what you will do if the worst happens; have a Plan B and a Plan C ready.
- Get the education you need to compete in your field; stay current.
- Save money. Don't spend foolishly. Aspire to be independent.
- Network. Meet people, make connections, and make memories.

Lisanne Glew
Leader of an Executive Compensation and Wealth Management Practice

I was an executive with a Canadian bank and decided to move off the executive track to the mommy track. I wanted to spend time with my young children instead of having a nanny raise them. My husband was offered a position in Richardson, Texas, so we decided to take advantage of the opportunity to allow me to stay home with our children for a few years. One of the benefits of moving to Texas was that the financial circumstances were positive with a lower cost of living as compared to Canada.

After four busy years at home, I decided to go back into the workforce in a role that would be professionally challenging and would also allow me to achieve some life–work balance. I wanted my children to understand that both parents can work and still be good parents. I wanted to be a role model for what is likely to be their future.

I have a law degree and an MBA, and finance is my expertise. So I joined a financial services company to build a wealth management practice where I could advise executives and their families on strategies to achieve their financial goals.

When you get off the track, you often don't reenter at the same level of compensation. There was a price, albeit not as big as some families face, but it was a financial step backward nonetheless. However, I had a plan and knew that as a wealth manager, my practice would be scalable. My vision was that I would be able to grow my practice as the children grew older and became more independent. And that's what has happened. It's great when plans work out, although life certainly doesn't always go according to plan!

When our kids were ages eight and ten, I found out I had breast cancer. This was a challenge for my family and my clients. I manage my clients' portfolios and their financial future, and they needed to know someone was at the wheel. You can't lose their confidence in you as their advisor, even when you have a trusted personal relationship. I was so blessed that my clients were very supportive. I disclosed my condition and assured them I was fine and on the road to recovery.

I had never had that level of personal disclosure with people or the ability to share just enough but not too much. Most of my clients are male executives, so I tried to be short and sweet with them. It was gratifying how supportive they were. Later on I became a resource for their wives, some of whom were experiencing cancer themselves. So out of a challenging experience came the opportunity to help others, which, I think, is an extremely important part of life's journey.

Now my practice focus has changed, so I work with more professional women than men. Women often choose to work with women with whom they have a trusted relationship. Women look at money differently than men. They manage risk and do their homework before working with an advisor; they conduct due diligence. Men play golf with one another and get involved in a lot of activities, but women want to get to know you on a personal level—that's part of their research.

Women look seriously at your pedigree, your credentials. From a financial perspective, they are more interested in managing risk. They aren't afraid to talk about longevity, so the conversation extends to insurance programs. Women want to get it out on the table and discuss the worst-case scenarios and how they're going to manage, whereas men often don't like to contemplate their demise.

If women are worried about financial risk, I advise them not to leave their financial health in someone else's hands. It's extremely important for women to get involved in their household financial management and not to assume their husbands or someone else have everything under control. They should have a working knowledge of their household cash flows and investments, and an understanding of what the outlook might be for job uncertainty for themselves and, if they're married, for their husbands. They should inform themselves.

For executives, there's more complexity in the compensation structure. Working with their advisor, they need to understand the various moving parts, including 401(k) plans, stock and insurance programs, and get a good feel for where and how various parts of their wealth are situated.

Women need to recognize that employment, careers, and even marriages have periods of transition. Things can change quickly, so when you are earning, you need to be saving. The younger you are, the more growth you will experience in your wealth if you start saving early.

Over time, you may face job changes, illness, and market declines, so you may not have as much as you think you will have. The important thing is to have a flexible plan and to work with people you can trust: people who have the skills and capabilities to be your guide, and who have the stamina to support you over the long term. Together you can take advantage of all the potential the future holds.

Sherri's Tips:
Achieving Financial Health

I am going to ask you to differentiate your wants from your needs and really clarify how they enforce or hurt the vision you have for yourself. This will entail taking an honest look at what you think makes you happy and how items you've amassed over the years have affected your financial and emotional well-being. Let's start by making two important distinctions. Needs are what you require to survive; wants are everything else, including the things you *think* you require to survive or make yourself feel good. Entitlements are often misguided beliefs we carry about what we think we have the *right* to have or own. There's definitely something to be said for needs that enhance our quality of life. But all too often we let a sense of entitlement vandalize a decent amount of reasonable wants.

Your Financial Health Checklist

√ I balance my bank statement every month.

√ I always pay my bills on time.

√ I live debt-free or have a plan to get there.

√ I contribute to my savings account consistently.

√ I pay my credit card balances off in full every month.

√ I pay my taxes on time.

√ I do not lose sleep at night over money issues.

√ I live well within my means.

√ I always carry cash for emergencies.

√ When I feel financially full, I share my wealth with others.

How did you do? Which statements are not true for you? Don't waste another minute—start a plan of action to improve your financial health!

"Haughtiness goes before destruction; humility precedes honor."
—*Proverbs 18:12* NLT

7

The Power
of Yes
and No

"Never allow a person to tell you no,
who doesn't have the power to say yes."
—Eleanor Roosevelt

They say when you want something done, give the job to the busiest person you know, and it will get done. Wonder how many times people have thought of you that way? One of the best ways to rebalance your life is to assess where and how you spend your time. If you don't have time for the people or activities you want, you're letting something else sit at the head of your table.

Sherri Elliott-Yeary

In order to feed our internal flames, we must wake up and make each of our choices consciously, with awareness. A conscious choice reflects our highest commitments and is in direct alignment with our vision for our lives. When we make conscious

In memory of Denise Vadala

choices, we take into consideration the effect our actions will have on our lives as a whole. We take the time to reflect on where our choices will lead us and the impact they will have on our future.

Every time we slip into unconscious decision making and forget about our deepest desires, we fall into an automatic trance, collapsing into whatever programming or patterns exist from our past. This trance is like going on autopilot: it takes no effort, no thinking. This trance whispers in our ears, "It doesn't matter. Just one more time. I'll start tomorrow, it's OK, no one will know." The voice of this trance encourages us to take the easy way out. "No worries!" it cries, as we turn off the road of our dreams and down the circular pathway of our past.

When we are not powerfully aware and making conscious choices, we fail to see the consequences of our actions. We blindly go about our days, never considering the long-term vision of our lives. If you make a list of some of your past choices in an area of your life where you haven't gotten the results you desired, you'll undoubtedly discover you have been asleep at the wheel. Somehow you've forgotten your future is determined by the actions you take today, by powerfully choosing to say yes or no and getting off autopilot.

Last year I took the opportunity to "fire a client" who I really enjoyed working with and who paid well. In this economy, that was a tough choice to make. I realized after a year of on-site partnering with the business owner, I had accomplished my role as a consultant and advisor and it was time to say, "Now you're ready to walk without me."

I spent the first month off reviewing the services I offered, choosing which ones I personally felt passionate about, and which ones I preferred to outsource. This process took time, energy, and honesty, but was well worth the investment. As a result, I decided I wanted to spend more time coaching women to achieve their personal best and educating organizations on the importance of generational differences. I am passionate about supporting and teaching companies the tools that allow them to better understand their most important asset: their people.

Once I had my blueprint, I identified where I needed support: virtual assistant, accountant, webmaster, editor, public relations, etc. I brought a team together that could support my vision. I took back my life by taking back my schedule. I make each appointment, so I do not overbook myself and have nothing left for soul-nourishing time with my husband, family, and myself. What happens then is that I am actually present and fully engaged with less stress since I no longer allow myself to run on empty.

A lot of people ask me, "Sherri, do you prefer to be at home or on the road speaking?" Wherever I am is where I want to be. If I don't have fun wherever I am, I'm spending a substantial amount of time in the wrong mind-set.

For women who passionately live an authentic life, a totally balanced day is not only unachievable, it's undesirable and boring. Yet I do strive for a balanced life. As I write this book, I'm working twelve-hour days so I can spend quality time with my husband when it's finished.

Only you know when your life feels off balance. Your personal and professional lives are clashing and you feel little satisfaction in anything you do. Your inner fire has died or is almost gone. Your intuitive vision is a past and distant memory and you are now on autopilot. Because we as women are good at disguising it, your boss or family may not notice you're overwhelmed. I suggest that the happiest people are the most passionate—not the most balanced, but we are living *big*!

Dr. Eileen Dowse

Executive Leadership Counselor and Trainer

I've never really tried to "have it all;" instead I've done my best to "manage it all." At the start of my career, I had three children all under the age of three. This was a period in my life in which I had to decide on my priorities. How much time and energy was I going to commit to motherhood? And how much time and energy was I going to commit to my career?

Just as my career got going, my family and I moved to a different country. This provided me another opportunity to "manage it all." I had to get the family settled, find a new client base, and create a reputation in the area I worked in.

After ten successful years, our oldest son had a terrible accident; a fifty-pound tree limb fell on his head, leaving him unconscious for three days. The odds were not in his favor.

Again, I was being called to make choices and be innovative in seeing the opportunities in everything around me. My life was challenging me to take a stand for what I am passionate about. Between rehab and a passion for not accepting mediocrity, our son completely recovered and continues to be successful in his career. As for me, riding out this chaos, I stayed focused and disciplined on balancing work and family and in my belief in the service I was providing to clients.

Once my life settled a bit, I recognized the need to have a PhD to help position myself in the market. I didn't have much time to devote to this, so I decided to go full throttle and accomplish the task quickly and efficiently. My hope was to have as little disruption in my life as possible. I had alerted my friends and family to what I was doing and the timeline I had created.

Having a completion date in mind helped me achieve my goal of completing my PhD in two and a half years. I later learned this was one of the most efficient completion times ever achieved. For me, it was about staying focused on my goal and making every decision and action relate to the task at hand. I suspect this is one of the secrets to having it all.

After twenty years since our last move, my husband (who was the president of a company) was placed in a position at work to choose between endorsing and conducting unethical, criminal behavior by the CEO or reporting the acts of treason to the FBI. He reported the crime to the FBI and was demoted; eventually he had to resign from the company. Our family received death threats, and we had to spend many hours providing witness statements to the FBI. Once again the opportunity to stand up for my values was being tested. Now, with only one wage earner (me) in the family, three kids in college, and huge financial responsibilities, it was time to rise to the occasion and not be victims of circumstance.

This twist and turn in our life led to another move, and again I was called to continue serving existing clients and build a reputation in my new location.

Just when I thought I had reached a plateau of stability, my mother began to suffer from Alzheimer's disease. This terrible disease is not for the weak of heart. I have begun to appreciate the expression "gut-wrenching," because going through that experience was like someone sticking their hand in my stomach, grabbing my guts, then twisting and pulling their hand out again. To complicate this issue, my mother lived in another country. This meant coordinating her care with siblings, having constant contact with caregivers, and making regular trips to help support the process. She passed away with the family knowing we did the best we possibly could do for her.

There must be something about stress, strain, and opportunity that start my motivational juices flowing because this last move and the illness of my mother got me focused on writing a second book, this one on leadership. That book is now finished, and with an aggressive new goal of writing four more books in one year, I know I will get it done. I suspect this is another secret in "having it all." You have to believe you can!

If I was to examine how I managed it all, I would say I have a knack for redirecting my energy and thoughts to make things happen and enjoy the process while doing it. Anyone can be sad, miserable, and annoying. Who benefits from that? I am often heard saying, "Just because you have a pain doesn't mean you need to be one." I believe there is a bright spot in everything, there is a lesson to be learned, and there's an opportunity to impact another life in a positive way. We all have a chance in this life to leave a legacy. In the end, that's all we can do: leave a legacy.

Whether I am with a client, my family, or my friends, I am there in the moment. My head is not focused on the many other things going on in my life. I stay focused and disciplined to achieve my goals, while at the same time I can have a good laugh and see the humor in the chaos that pops up when you least expect it.

What are my strategies for saying yes and no? I keep life simple. I don't accumulate "stuff" because then I will have to manage "stuff." Instead I value those precious moments and times I have with people. I am grateful and appreciative of everything that appears in my life. Everything that comes my way is an opportunity, and I get to choose how I want to approach it.

Life is really about perspective, the choices we make, and what we do with what is given to us. If I've learned anything in my life, I've learned to stay open to possibilities and see a positive in everything that happens to me. When I get into bed at the end of the day, I am at peace. I know I have seized the day, and even if chaos jumped in for a visit, I embrace it with open arms and continue to keep my focus on my goal while dancing with chaos through the process.

I have it all, and tomorrow I will have the opportunity to have more!

Tips by Dr. Eileen Dowse: Dealing with Stress

How can you get rid of stress? Living in a world without stress isn't the answer. Life would either be very dull, or you would be unconscious. The issue isn't how to get rid of stress, but how to manage it, and the best way is to check your PULSE.

P: Plan your time and get organized.
- Set priorities with timelines for the tasks you want to complete.
- Make a weekly schedule spacing out your activities and balancing your obligations.
- Avoid procrastination—do it, dump it, or delegate it.

U: Understand the situation.

- Step back and view the situation from a different vantage point; gaining the big picture is key to understanding how to manage any situation.
- Evaluate which activities (both mental and physical) are depleting your energy. Make some choices about what to keep and what to remove.

L: Let loose and be positive.

- Get happy. It's been proven that happier people live longer, have fewer physical problems, and are more productive. Manage your stress by enjoying your life.
- Replace criticism with encouragement. Motivate yourself with choice, not fear.
- Choose. Your happiness (or misery) depends upon what you tell yourself, how you treat yourself, and how you interpret your world. Take a more positive approach to life.

S: Surround yourself with a good support network.

- Question if your current support system is a help or a hindrance. Choose people who can be of benefit to you.
- Form a network of people (mentors, coaches, friends, and confidants) who can help provide the resources and perspectives you need.

E: Exercise and stay healthy.

- Exercise your body. Your health and productivity depend upon your body's ability to bring oxygen and food to its cells.
- Eat a balanced diet.
- Sleep seven to eight hours a night, allowing your brain and body to get the rest and repair it needs.

Managing stress is an "inside job." I encourage you to check your PULSE rate regularly and enjoy the opportunities in store for you.

Karen Hunt

Executive Marketing Director for a
Drug and Alcohol Treatment Organization

I grew up in dysfunctional family. My father drank heavily and my mother was a victim of domestic violence. I decided to get out as soon as possible by graduating at age sixteen. When I turned seventeen, my sister died in a car accident while drinking and driving.

I started cosmetology school and married at age eighteen, but my husband had cancer and passed away. I was a widow at age nineteen.

I had taken a sabbatical from school to care for my husband, so after he passed away, I finished cosmetology school, completed an internship, and then opened my own salon. I was twenty years old.

When I was twenty-four, my parents divorced, and it hit me hard. It made me believe you can't take anything for granted. I prayed a lot and dove into my new business. I didn't really have a teenage life, so I got a little wild in my twenties. My mother came and talked to me, and that talk straightened me out. I thought, *This is not how I want to live my life. I want to be productive and successful.*

I'm a firm believer in perseverance and hard work. It is my belief that for women to have a healthy amount of self-esteem and confidence, we need to invest in ourselves and not expect to be fed through only our love interest or another person.

Trust, honesty, good morals, and values are important. Many people talk about happiness but are not able to make the changes necessary to achieve success in being happy. In my opinion, to be happy and healthy means a lot, but living it every day is crucial.

I believe that we can give and receive love through a higher power; it's very important to me that I have this connection. I wish I had connected with a spiritual mentor, but instead I learned my lessons the hard way. I wasn't able to enjoy my childhood and have fun, so now I live life every day to the fullest.

My advice to other women is to love yourself first, and to slow down. Life is not going to end if you don't get married at age twenty. There's so much to accomplish in life. You can't tell your heart what to do, but you can tell it to wait. As women, we have a tendency to put our lives on hold for others' needs, but we can wind up forgetting what we really want from life. I believe things happen for a reason and we meet the right people at the right time and that's part of why I do what I do.

The company I work with markets addiction treatment programs to medical professionals, therapists, hospitals, ERs, psych units, clergy, family attorneys, and consumers. When you start talking about alcohol and drug addiction, it spurs a reaction in anyone who has been touched by addiction. We're starting an initiative with clergy and educating them to tell their church members that it's OK to say, "I have a problem and I need help."

I feel God has put me where I need to be right now. I try to assist families so they can take the next step in getting help toward recovery. There is support and help for people experiencing addiction; no matter where you are today, there is a better place. Don't lose hope. There's a better life out there, one with options, but those seeking help have to ask. There is someone who can walk us through life in recovery.

Tere Bettis

Human Resources Business Partner

I have always been the one to try to control everything, including myself and my family, in "having it all." Now, I know I can't really control anything in front of my nose, but that didn't keep me from trying! At a certain point in my life, I didn't really have a career. We had the trappings of the good life, but in reality, we were just going through the motions.

My dad was sick for over a year before being diagnosed with prostate cancer. Once diagnosed, he only lived a few months longer. It was very hard on my mother. She took care of him day and night and made herself sick in the process.

As I was growing up, my father's career often took him on the road. As soon as school was out, we were all in the car for the entire summer. I looked up to my dad and was so proud of being his daughter when we traveled together. I got to visit many cities and states and made numerous friends whom I am blessed to count as friends today.

I remember when I was about sixteen years old my father telling me that he *knew* that there was a God because of the events or happenings he had seen in this life. I was a teenager and had not yet experienced life's twists and turns and, while I took him at his word, I could not relate to my father's perspective.

My dad and mom made a striking couple. Many times, when we were in stores, customers would think he was the store manager and ask him for assistance. I knew then that the way you dressed and presented yourself said something to the world about you.

Dad was a supporter of my career early on. He taught me the importance of building relationships and always said, "You can never have too many friends." I'm blessed to have a few close friends whom I know I can call and count on for anything.

My dad wanted me to be able to take care of myself by myself, no matter what happened around me. He made me believe in myself and my abilities. He was my rock and, when he died, my rock was gone.

I've been fortunate to have the support of my husband, Lonny. This year we will celebrate thirty-eight years of marriage. Anyone who has been married that long knows there are ups and downs, but having his support to raise our daughter is a blessing.

I learned the importance of looking in the mirror that others are holding up for you and seeing things from their perspective. I learned it can be hard to look in that mirror. But when I do look and accept what others see, I grow in ways I would not be able to with only my own perspective.

Patience and faith are the two most important things I can share with others. Patience, because we can't have it all right now, but if we are persistent, open, supportive, and available, we will have what we need. Faith, because, as my father told me he had, I have now seen enough to know there is a God. I am grateful to have lived long enough to understand what my father meant. Each day I ask God for the strength, courage, and will to carry out His plan in my life. I ask that He reveal to me each day the people I need to meet and the opportunity to reflect His love and strength. I have seen miracles in daily living and tragedies no one can understand. Through it all, I know He walks with me, carries me when I am unable to move forward, and leads me if I let Him.

Sherri's Tips:
Decide to Say Yes or No

It's natural to make the wrong decision sometimes. We learn from our mistakes, so don't get too upset about saying yes to the wrong thing and no to the right thing. Sometimes it can be very hard to choose the right path, but there are ways to make your decisions more wisely.

- **Think about what you are going to do before you do it.** You can let your passions motivate you, but you also have to consider the practicality of your decisions. What is the best way to accomplish what you want? What approach keeps hurt feelings or other consequences to a minimum? When you choose to say yes or no, your actions impact others, but you have to do what's right for *you*.
- **Avoid rash decisions.** Don't do something in the heat of the moment. Wait until you are calm and relaxed before you make the final decision, and then do something about it. It's a good idea to confide in someone and get some feedback on what you could do, but keep in mind that it's your decision.
- **Don't overthink.** Don't stress over small decisions that won't impact your life in significant ways. Overthinking everything can cause stress, which is bad for you.

- **Trust yourself.** Go with your gut, but always think through any big and crucial decision. Have faith in yourself and in your instincts. After all, the only person who truly can advise you is you.

> *"Such things were written in the Scriptures long ago to teach us. And the Scriptures give us hope and encouragement as we wait patiently for God's promises to be fulfilled."*
> —Romans 15:4 NLT

8

Live an Empowered
Life and
Follow Your Passion

"Great dancers are not great because of their technique;
they are great because of their passion."
—Martha Graham

*Passions can be energizing and fill you with joy. If you don't have passion in
your life, give yourself permission to let it out and live life fully.*

Sherri Elliott-Yeary

What does it mean to be empowered? To empower means to
give or add power to propel. When you're empowered, you feel
strong, alive, and clear, with a vibrant energy that runs through
your body. When you make choices that empower you, you are
thrust into the present moment. You experience a deep inner
peace knowing that you are exactly where you need to be.
When you feel empowered, you have access to higher levels of

consciousness. Because you are choosing to move forward in a powerful way, your mind is quiet and void of its usual negative chatter.

People who live an empowered life stand up for themselves and invite others to do the same. They are in a state of being in pure love. They have a love of life, self, and others. They provide hope to those who shrink in the presence of everyday life. People who feel empowered are natural leaders who inspire those around them. Ask yourself the question, "Does this choice empower me or does it disempower me?" This will quickly move you out of the past and into the present moment, because you can actually *feel* the experience of empowerment inside your body. You know that your choices empower you when they leave you feeling strong and secure inside.

It's time to let go of the "I can't" excuses. Yes, even busy women can find the time to do something they love. When the moment presents itself, enjoy the adventure. If you're tempted to allow "more important" tasks to replace this spot on your calendar, don't.

We have all mastered the art of thinking our way to nowhere. We can dwell, ponder, and rationalize all we want, but if we wind up taking an action that leaves us weak and disempowered, we have diminished our life-sustaining energy, and we take a step back from our desired goals.

Maybe you've noticed your emotions fluctuate constantly. Therefore, it's not the wisest idea to navigate by them. If you want to arrive at your desired destination, I suggest you forget about your emotions for a while. Don't use them as your compass for your future; they weren't designed for that. As long as you allow your emotions to be your single guide, you forfeit your right to achieve your goals and live the life you desire.

Taking the high road and making the right choices may not always feel comfortable. In fact, it may feel very uncomfortable to make a choice outside the predictability and familiarity of your past. It might be difficult not to go shopping, or to stay with your exercise program. If you do something different from what you've been doing for the past ten or twenty years, it will very likely feel scary. But once you can see that changing your habits will leave you feeling empowered and strong, you can consciously decide which path you want to take.

A moment of perfection comes when we give ourselves the gift of empowering choice, a conscious choice that is consistent with our deepest desires. Each of us has the ability to create a lifetime of perfect moments simply by following a life that gives us energy and peace.

Passions are lived out in as many ways as there are women. Your passions are inside you, and they will reveal themselves if you allow them to.

Sitting on my desk is a sign that reads, "ARE YOU OVER YOUR SKIS?" I keep it there as a reminder of what empowerment feels like. Being empowered is similar to the feeling of exhilaration that comes from moving effortlessly down a mountain. It is a state of being in balance with the laws of nature where you are giving all that you have, not holding on, not looking back, but staying keenly focused on where you want to go. For those of you who aren't skiers, one thing you quickly learn when you start skiing is that if your weight is not over your skis, you will be thrown off balance.

While I was on vacation in Banff, Canada, I was preparing for an upcoming speech and realized that I didn't want to share my usual message. I felt compelled to share what I've learned with other women, and it took time and commitment to disconnect from the busyness in my life, sit quietly, and receive the message of what I wanted to say.

Friends and family who know me well know that patience is not my strongest skill, but I am working on it daily. I have learned that if I do not humble myself, God will keep giving me opportunities (in other words, problems) to get it right.

I decided that my new speech was really a book in the making. Once I decided to turn it into a book, I notified my husband, clients, and friends that I had a new passion. I felt so strongly about sharing this book with my readers, I knew I would have to make sacrifices if I wanted the book to be the best it could be. I cut back on my normal spending and used savings to pay for expenses related to publishing the book.

We all know there is no magic formula for prosperity and happiness, but there's one common denominator I've found among successful women: they are passionate and driven to do what they do. They're on fire. An inner spark in the mind, spirit, and soul burns intensely, driving them over seemingly insurmountable barriers. Passionate women don't do what they do just because they can; they do it because they are irresistibly compelled.

I did not grow up dreaming of being an author or business owner. I grew up dreaming of having the ability to live life on my terms. I'm thankful each day when I wake up excited about life and the opportunities yet to be discovered. If I didn't follow my path and share my vision with others, a piece of the puzzle of my life would be missing.

We as women have endurance challenges. Anytime we feel overwhelmed or on the verge of defeat, every step can seem an enormous effort, every minor conflict an obstacle. Yet a small change of action can make a huge difference. One toe inches forward, then another, and before long you have taken a stride past the obstacle, a stride that you once thought would never happen.

Before long, you are following your passion and achieving miracles.

Maura Schreier-Fleming
Consultant and Corporate Trainer Specializing in Sales

What did you want when you started your career? Was it excitement? Maybe it was being part of a talented team. Hopefully you loved the work! But perhaps you only wanted the paycheck. If that's the case, you may be limiting your career success. Just bringing home a paycheck isn't enough to create the joy you should have in your career.

I was lucky. I had been in college selling raffle tickets for my sorority when I discovered my career. I remember talking with another student who wasn't interested in buying my tickets. Instead of giving up, I remember saying something (unfortunately I can't remember now what I said) that made him look at me and say, "OK. I'll take four." Obviously, I was destined to be in sales. But what would I sell?

During the summer of my junior year, I was accepted into a retail training program at a department store in the ladies' clothing department. There were women who had worked there for more than thirty years. They could tell you before a customer approached the counter what that person would buy. In almost every single case, they were right. It was interesting that these women lacked a formal education yet they could outsell management every time.

As it turned out, these same women—who were generating the store's revenue—weren't getting paid well for their efforts, nor were they respected for their work. I found that disconcerting. Retail just wasn't for me.

Then I found a product to love, and my career in sales began in earnest. You, too, will be much happier and more successful if you look at what you enjoy and love and seek work that allows you to follow those passions. If you don't know what you like, there are ways to determine your strengths. For example, I knew a woman who played as a child organizing her closets. Now, she is a successful time-management consultant. The love of order and organization she had as a child became a big part of her work as an adult. It brings her joy.

Think about your childhood. If you start with your passion, your purpose will follow. It's the best way to build a career.

Do you wake up feeling energized or do you have a feeling of dread at the thought of the day ahead? A good rule of thumb is that if you like what you do, it doesn't feel like work. I think it's better to start with what you love instead of having to create your dream job. But even if you love your work, that's not enough for your life. You've got to have passion in your life. How do you do that?

Ask yourself, what brings you joy? Do you have it on your schedule? When you put the activity that brings you joy into your calendar, you'll be more likely to do it. Life without joy is no life.

Only you can bring the joy you want into your life.

Anne Spoon

Artist Who Paints Portraits, Still Lifes, and Landscapes

Painting is my passion. From a very early age, I used drawing as a creative outlet. Then, in high school, at about age fifteen, my art teacher introduced me to oil painting. I was hooked! I'm fortunate that I knew what I wanted to do in life from this very young age. Yet I understand that finding one's passion does not always come easily; sometimes it has to be uncovered, then nurtured.

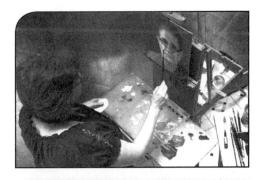

When I graduated from art school, I rewarded myself with a getaway to an old, Russian resort in New York. The Russian architecture included a teardrop shaped roof and a church; the resort was situated on one hundred acres. I remember the resort fondly, as it is where I met my husband.

Larry, who was from Oklahoma, was renting a

room at the resort and enjoying the relaxing environment. He didn't like New York and desired to go back home to Oklahoma. After we married, he stayed in New York with me for five years. Finally, I gave in to his desire to move home and agreed to move to Oklahoma. By this time, he knew what he was getting into: he had married an artist who just had to paint.

Although I moved for love, I also had the opportunity to paint full-time. Because the cost of living was much lower in Oklahoma than in New York, I did not need to take another job. One of the first things I told my husband in that old, Russian resort was, "I have to paint! If I don't, I'm difficult to live with. I have to do it. It's just part of who I am." He listened.

Larry has been so supportive; he honors my passion to paint and has allowed me to cultivate my craft. I have painted ever since, and I have been able to raise our children without having to take a full-time job.

Why is painting my passion? I believe it's a gift from God. It's about creating something beautiful from blankness. This world is so full of ugliness and hate; I believe I was put here to bring something beautiful to it. I feel that if I didn't nurture this gift, it would be a direct insult to God.

Can passion be developed? Certainly. I think many people are searching for their passion, but have a hard time finding it. My advice is to discover what you enjoy. Passion can be found in a weekend project, by serving on a local committee, or by helping others in need. It's OK to try many things to find your passion; you have to expose yourself to so much to find what you like. It does not have to be your full-time work to be rewarding. Sometimes sacrifices need to be made. My family sacrifices so I can paint. We could have had more things if I was working at a different job, but the reality is I could go out and get a job and be miserable. For me, a bad day painting is better than a good day working.

A creative career like mine can be hit or miss too. Some years are better than others; our current economy has provided quite the roller coaster ride. Yet it's a sacrifice that love has made: my family's love for me and my love to paint. My kids have learned much by watching me go through success *and* failure. It is so important for them. I want them to follow their gifts and work doing something they enjoy. I hope they find the same gratification in their pursuits.

Recently I was diagnosed with lupus; this has really slowed me down. As a wife and mother, I have many obligations in addition to my paintings. However, I now have limited energy and a lot of pain. I'm able to slowly come to the studio for a couple of hours and pace myself. I'm learning to control stress. Stress makes the lupus flare up, rendering me unable to paint. Yet it hasn't stopped me from enjoying my passion. When I'm able to paint, I enjoy it as much as ever—if not more.

As women, wives, and mothers, we love our families and tirelessly tend to their needs. However, we also must nurture ourselves and embrace our gifts. It's important. It is not selfish to take time for yourself and replenish your cup. It is why I went to the Russian resort. From there, my passion has not only come to life, it has become my life. And I couldn't be happier.

Eve Mayer Orsburn
Social Media Strategist

I have come to learn that I'm terrible at working for other people. My ideas are typically a bit outrageous, and I don't always agree with other people's opinions. I believe in a hardworking, extremely fun, and open work environment.

This is the reason I love social media. It's transparent. If someone is doing a bad job, they shouldn't be surprised to be let go. If they're doing a great job, they should be rewarded. My biggest weaknesses are keeping my life in balance and trusting myself to make the right decisions and to take care of myself without question or guilt. I am on my own schedule, but my family time—spending time with my daughter and husband—is my greatest opportunity for happiness. That's where the joy comes from.

Running a company is extremely exciting and fulfilling, but I think family and friends are also very important. A lot of times a professional woman struggles to take care of herself and her family. It's a struggle to fit in time for friendships and family, so I try to do a good job at that.

There are times when something overtakes the other things and I lose the balance, so I have to be constantly honest with myself. If I see a weakness in myself, I try to get better. If I screw up, I don't try to hide it. I share it and use it as a teaching opportunity.

If you want to start your own business, be prepared for years of potential anxiety, but have courage and don't let that stop you. Find a mentor, someone who has the life that you want. Look at your potential mentor as a whole person: Is she happy with her personal life as well as her business life?

If an idea keeps gnawing at you, there's something to it. If it's just a tough day, keep on going.

I do know a lot of women who have fantastic ideas but don't ask for help, so they don't get what they want. Or it takes a really long time for their dream to come to fruition. The more you help people, the more you feel comfortable asking for help.

I've been in media a long time, both in radio and music marketing, and I have found that traditional advertising methods just aren't working anymore. My social media company is one of many companies I have started. I've always been an entrepreneur and I love it.

Today we have an office in Paris and representatives in eight cities. We aren't the largest social media company, but we are one of the most respected, and that's what's important. I don't have a perfect life, but my life is perfect for me.

Sherri's Tips: Discover Your Passion

- **Connect with your early interests.** Can you recall a pleasant childhood memory of playing? What did you love to do? Chances are what you love to do today grew roots in what you loved to do then.

- **Acknowledge your current interests.** Imagine you have all the money you need and twelve months to do anything and everything you want to do. You could pursue any career or hobby, live in a new place, sing with your favorite band, or climb Mount Everest. What would you choose to do?

- **Make choices.** As choices are presented to you, pay attention to your responses. Reject whatever leaves you cold, even if it pays more money or makes someone else happy.

- **Give yourself permission to change your life.** We all go through stages where our energy comes from a particular source. Once that source no longer provides a driving vitality, it is OK to let go and ignite a new fire.

- **Be willing to pay the price.** You may want to follow your passion, but you also must be prepared for the costs. Going back to school or starting a new business may mean using your savings or going into debt. Be prepared for the challenges and sacrifices you must make to follow your dream.

"I believe in your commands; now teach me
good judgment and knowledge."
—Psalm 119:66 NLT

9

Recognizing
Opportunities

"Do something every day that scares you."
—Eleanor Roosevelt

When you go on any journey, you'll encounter detours and obstacles as well as green lights and HOV lanes. How do you tell the difference between what's valuable and what's not valuable on your journey toward having it all? Ask yourself how you typically handle roadblocks: Do you go around, over, or through them? Or do you give up without trying? Seeing opportunities within roadblocks is key to getting them out of your way and where they belong— behind you.

Sherri Elliott-Yeary

Every important choice we make is being guided by one of two sources: either it is an act of faith or it is an act of fear. Faith opens the door to a new future. It allows us to take new routes and

explore different avenues. When we are grounded in faith, we have the courage to travel to destinations we've never visited. This is an extremely potent question: "Is this an act of faith or is it an act of fear?" This question supports us in making choices from our highest selves, from the part of us that is deeply connected to all that is and all that will be. When we are making choices that are sourced by our spiritual essence and are grounded in faith, we experience unbounded freedom.

We must ask ourselves, "Where is my faith right now? Is my faith in my fears? Am I placing my faith in the idea that I'm not going to get what I want? Or am I placing my faith in the perfection of God and His plan for me? Do I have faith that I will be given the ability to recognize opportunities?"

Most of us misplace our faith. We have more faith in our pain, our past, and our negative beliefs than we do in our innate right to be happy.

When we choose to live a faith-based life, our first task is to submit ourselves to the general manager of the universe known to me as God. Faith asks us to surrender control of our lives. To surrender affirms that we trust a higher power to tend to our needs, show us the opportunities we have in our life, and guide us in the right direction. To surrender is an act of faith; it's a gift that you give yourself.

The truth releases us from the grip of our past. When we tell the truth, even if we don't like the fact that we have been overcommitted to something other than what we say we've been striving for, we are liberated from our internal struggle. A beautiful Russian proverb states, "The bitter truth is better than a sweet lie." Our pain and suffering come from perpetuating the lie by insisting, "I'm committed to having an intimate relationship," "I'm committed to being in great physical health," or "I'm committed to building my company and having a thriving career!" when we are, in fact, deeply committed to something else. When we tell the truth—that we're really committed to something other than what we've been saying we are—our suffering subsides.

By exposing those subconscious commitments we gain the freedom to stand in the truth. Then we have the strength to be honest and say, "I've wanted an intimate relationship with a partner who will love, honor, and adore me."

I had been married before and had not been truthful with myself with respect to my bad partner-picking; I either chose men who were not emotionally available or men who were too available for others. When I married my husband, Mason, I had faith that God placed him in my life for a reason. I was thrilled that he had two daughters, Meredith and Jessica, as I had Khirsten, who was similar in age. The addition of his girls gave me an opportunity to connect with them on a different level than their birth mother, because we are very different women.

Within the first three months of our marriage, Mason and I sat down to discuss our financial obligations as a newly married couple and the parents of three girls in their twenties. Neither Mason nor I had ever partnered with our prior spouses on financial matters; we were both independent decision makers and it was foreign to us to consult with a spouse on financial issues. While his two girls were at college, Mason had his office manager pay the girls' bills. He didn't open them and was unaware of what they were spending each month. As Mason states, he "took the path of least resistance by taking care of his girls' bills, like a normal loving dad would want to do."

Using my financial degree for a change, I decided to analyze the girls' total spending per month, including the allowance they received from their father's business, to determine what our actual financial obligations were per month for all three of our girls. I wasn't surprised to discover Meredith and Jessica spent much more than their dad knew.

I already knew that, due to a long and unhealthy marriage, my husband's emotional needs were met by his relationship to his daughters. Mason taught the girls to ski, snowboard, surf, scuba dive, and more. He loved spending time with them; it brought him joy and happiness.

For most of us in the real world, no one pays our credit card bills for us, or pays for our mistakes, accidents, or oversights. It was up to me to take the unpopular stance with his girls in regard to our financial commitment. I took away their credit cards, and gave them gas cards instead. I had to coach my husband on what we needed to do as a couple to support the girls and empower them to be self-sufficient and informed young women who can stand on their own feet. They would never be able to become self-sufficient women if their dad is always rescuing them or over-providing for them.

Suffice it to say that I'm not the most popular stepmother, but I am OK with that as long as I know these difficult changes will ultimately help the girls. My greatest gift to Jessica and Meredith is to help them become the independent, dynamic women I know they have within them. They just need to be shown how.

When we find our own solutions, we grow stronger. Excessive reliance on others can weaken us. Soon we shy away from challenges we once might have conquered with relish and ease. My vocabulary does not include the word "failure;" I may need to alter my course of action and delay my expectations, but I don't give up. I'm ever mindful of how sweet it is to reach the top of the mountain.

I want Mason's girls to feel that same exhilarating sense of accomplishment and joy that comes only when you've done something great using your own steam.

Shelly Little
CEO

When I was a young adult I had an amazing opportunity to live overseas for several years and experience many different cultures in a way I had never even conceived possible. Since I was an expatriate, I was insulated, but I was blessed to be given opportunities to get to know the local people, get involved in local community organizations, and have my eyes opened to the realities of what the majority of the world population faces daily.

In conjunction with becoming a Christian, I experienced a wake-up call. Everything came into sharper focus for me and inspired a need for me to do something to give back to others. I became intentional in finding causes that would give me opportunities to help in a variety of ways. I also sought out a church that would allow me to connect with people who cared about the community in which I lived.

I felt it important to be purposeful in what I invested my time in, including taking on challenges that forced me to go outside of my comfort zone, to challenge my assumptions, and to push myself physically and mentally, personally, and professionally.

More than ever before, I learned how important it is to live in the moment, appreciate what we do have, and tell those we love how we feel, without regret.

From my employees, I've learned the importance of giving them opportunities to stretch themselves and to be more understanding of failure when it is the result of good faith effort. These mistakes can result in breakthroughs if we learn from them. When you empower your employees, they know you trust them and want them to be successful. They've taught me so much and made me so very proud to know them and work with them.

In the past, I shied away from opportunities that could result in my making a mistake, but now I realize we can actually feel a sense of accomplishment when overcoming an obstacle. I've learned that fear can be motivating.

The internal sense of knowing I was blessed to be in a position to help others grow to that next level and hold the safety net for them is part of what having it all means to me. The ability to support and watch others grow is tremendously satisfying.

My advice to others is to decide for yourself what "having it all" means to you. Don't let society define it for you. When you have faith and people who love and support you, you can take risks knowing you will survive and can thrive.

Kathy Light

Leadership Development Expert

Like many professional women now in their forties, I started my business career with the intention of growing professionally while somehow making a difference in the world. In 1995 I had my first child and he changed everything. I continued working full-time, all the while experiencing the daily guilt that comes with the working-mom territory, feeling like I could never do enough as a mom or as a professional.

Despite my guilt, I flourished in my career and continued to take on more responsibility, but the happiness of my family was always—and still is—my number one priority. Having spent most of my corporate career as a leadership development consultant and training director, I was able to easily transition to coaching and training leaders on a contract basis for several years. We had another child, and as the kids got older I gradually added to my client base. This career option allowed me to be home when the kids got out of school.

About half of my revenue came from contracts with my former employer, and, like so many corporations, budgets were sliced. The first casualty was leadership development. In addition, there was a significant downturn in my husband's business, a luxury decorative painting company.

Ever the optimist, I turned my attention to networking and relationship building to promote my business and to helping my husband keep his business afloat. In retrospect, I think I was expecting things to just fall into place for me, as they somehow always had.

While continuing to work with clients and generate new ones, I decided to pursue my dream to publish my first book, *Reasons Why YOU ROCK!* Since creating the book, I've delivered presentations, workshops, and retreats all around the Dallas–Fort Worth area based on its core message.

The book is about the importance of truly realizing your own greatness so your light can shine brightly in the world and inspire others to shine as well. I am passionate about this work.

Becoming an author has opened many doors for me and opened my eyes to many possibilities. It has helped me to think big again, with a crystal-clear focus on why I was put on this earth: to help people realize why they rock!

Sherri's Tips:
Recognizing Important Crossroads in Life

Life is full of many twists and turns. We make decisions that impact our future on a minute-by-minute basis. It's critical that we realize this and pay attention so we can make the right choices. Otherwise we might get sidetracked in a direction we don't want to go. It can happen in the blink of an eye.

You make hundreds, if not thousands, of seemingly small decisions every day. You decide when to get up, how to spend your time, and what to eat. Collectively, all these little choices add up to be your life. You don't even think about most decisions. You semiconsciously follow your habits, good or bad, living life on autopilot. This isn't an efficient way to live; you'd waste a lot of time if you analyzed every single choice every day. But you may pay a price in failing to recognize the *significance* of many of these so-called small crossroads. Some decisions require more thought. If you continually *wish* your life were different but do things the same old way, you'll get the same old result.

Let the little crossroad decisions remain on autopilot, but recognize that some decisions require more thought, strategy, and determination.

Here are a few helpful steps as you determine the right opportunities:

1. **Take responsibility for your actions.** Few of us like to be held accountable for the results in our lives, but if you don't start accepting this responsibility now, you will likely stay stuck right where you are. Acknowledge that you are the one who decides what you do today. You are the one who chooses:

- how you react to others;
- what you do with your time;
- how you spend your money;
- what and how much you eat;
- who you spend time with;
- what you say; and
- your attitude.

Each of these tiny little crossroads may need your attention. Start with the area most in need of improvement or a new direction.

2. **Don't play the victim.** Once you accept responsibility for your life, you have to accept that your circumstances are your own. Eliminate "I can't" from your vocabulary and stop blaming others for your mistakes.

If, today, you are stuck where you don't want to be, it isn't your spouse's fault, your boss's fault, your parents' fault, or the fault of anyone who wronged you in the past or present. These people may have played a part in making things more difficult for you, but it's up to you to move on. Stop feeling sorry for yourself and decide to take a new path. It's your responsibility to start making better choices that can lead to better results right now. If you are an adult, there is no reason that *you can't*.

3. **Choose a New Path.** Look at your life. What is the most troubling thing you face? What causes you the most grief? Is it a relationship, your finances, your job, or your health? Get laser-like focus on the problem that's keeping you from living the life you want, and look at the paths available to you for a new life.

Let's assume the major problem in your life right now is your job. Here are a few smart choices to make while you identify your true passion and calling:

- You chose to show up to work today; you have made a commitment and will honor your word.
- You chose not to quit, because it is easier to find a new opportunity when you are currently employed and learning new skills.
- You chose to get out of bed early and research job alternatives before you went to work.
- You chose to not buy lunch; instead, you bring your lunch to save money.
- You chose to not charge another unnecessary purchase to your credit card; this habit will help in reducing your debt so you will have the financial means to support your new passion.
- You chose to keep paying your bills so you build a positive credit rating.

These are all little crossroads you faced today that got you where you are right at this moment. Which choices do you need to change to get you started down a new path? Obviously, if you want to change jobs, you need to get out of bed, research alternatives, and stop spending money needlessly. Start adding new choices to help you reach your goal, like networking, brushing up your resume, going back to school, and more.

It's really simple: keep making the same choices and you get the same outcome. Change a few choices and you will find yourself moving past the crossroads to a new and better life.

"Guard your heart above all else,
for it determines the course of your life."
—*Proverbs 4:23* NLT

10

Better or Bitter—
The Choice
is Yours!

"Instead of getting bitter, we can recognize these times of
testing as opportunities to become better."
—Sherri Elliott-Yeary

*Life in this fallen world is full of injustices. A marriage you thought would
last forever could end in divorce. A business you worked hard to build could
fail, leaving you in financial ruin. A child you invested your life into could
make choices that grieve you deeply. An accident or serious illness could hit
you, even when you've been living a healthy lifestyle. Responding to life's
injustices with bitterness will only poison your soul. But when you choose to
let go of bitterness and trust God to help you move on, you heal no matter
what you've suffered.*

Sherri Elliott-Yeary

If you've ever been used, abused, deceived, misunderstood, forgotten, cheated on, or taken advantage of, you are a woman who knows what it's like to be "burned." Most of us have had some of these painful experiences in our lives at one time or another.

When I was twelve years old, my great-uncle, Neil, molested me, took away my childhood innocence, and left me unable to be comfortable in a man's presence until I married my husband. You see, I could not understand how a person could harm a child or why my parents did not protect me from him.

Both of my younger sisters were also sexually abused by our uncle and, today, neither is able to sustain a healthy marital relationship. Why do we hurt ourselves long after the offender has left? Why is it that we turn anger inward and continue to inflict pain on ourselves? Why do we overeat, hoping it will make us feel better when it only leaves us fat and unhealthy? Why do we overspend, buying things we don't need (and sometimes don't even take out of the box), seeking to numb the pain?

I have tried all of the above: I shopped and never wore most of what I bought to fill the void, and, until fourteen years ago, I used food when I needed comfort. The result of overeating created insulation around myself so men would not be attracted to me or look at me; it made me feel safe and protected.

I knew if I was ever going to free myself from childhood issues, I needed to take matters into my own hands and seek

help. Help came in many forms over the years; I read self-help books, worked with a faith-based therapist, and attended workshops. Honestly, the best healing work came from a place deep inside myself, once I was able and willing to acknowledge that I had a problem.

Because of healing work in my life, I can now look back at the hurtful actions I inflicted upon myself and put them where they belong—the past. I am no longer that young, helpless, chubby girl. I now have the resources, through my relationship with God and the power of His Word, to help me close the wounds of the past.

Through my marriage to Mason, I feel safe, protected, and able to understand the importance of forgiveness. When someone you care about hurts you, you can hold on to anger, resentment, and thoughts of revenge, or you can embrace forgiveness and move forward.

The reality is that there will always be people who irritate us and make us angry; we will never escape every rude, selfish, and unjust person. There will also be times when people whom we've trusted will disappoint us and let us down. Unfortunately it's almost impossible to be in relationships with people without sometimes getting hurt or offended.

If you've been hurt, you probably know that the typical first response is usually to get upset or become angry. Having negative emotions when we've been hurt is a natural inclination. I don't think it is a sin to *feel* negative emotions; it's a natural feeling.

I am so grateful God has provided a way for us to avoid becoming bitter when we've been hurt. He has given each of us the power of the Holy Spirit, including the fruit of self-control. Over time, and through experience, God develops in us the ability to control ourselves by operating in the fruit of self-control while leaning on Him. This means we just don't say and do whatever we are feeling at that moment. Exercising self-control is a choice we make as *our* part in dealing with negative emotions. But the power to release and forgive the offenses of others only comes from God; we simply can't do it in our own strength.

God does not want us to travel through life carrying the weight of past pains. He wants us to be women who enjoy our journey, free of excess baggage. I encourage you to be smart enough to stop hurting yourself after someone has hurt you.

Niesha Alexander

Virtual Assistant and Jewelry Designer

"The obstacles of your past can become the gateways that lead to new beginnings."
—Ralph Blum

Like many, I had my entire life perfectly mapped out: graduate from college, invest, save, purchase a home, get married, have kids, travel, retire, and travel more; all in that perfect order. My life caved in the moment my perfect plans began to unravel. My

Christian faith was shaken, my self-worth was questioned, and my future was unsure.

At nineteen, after just two years in college, I got married. A year later, I gave birth to my first child. I faced many difficult times in my marriage. Emotional, physical, spiritual, and financial abuse took their toll on me and I needed to make some changes. Four children and twelve years later, God provided a way of escape from my unhealthy marriage, which had nearly broken my spirit and destroyed my character. I call it my "Day of Freedom!"

While I do not condone divorce, I do support freedom from abusive relationships that destroy a person's well-being and inevitably destroy who they are. In Ephesians 6:12 the Bible says, "For we wrestle not against flesh and blood, but against principalities, against powers, against the rulers of the darkness of this world, against spiritual wickedness in high places." I knew the freedom I sought was not from a person, but from the oppression, depression, hopelessness, and discouragement I had endured for so many years. Understanding Ephesians 6:12 helped me escape my situation without bitterness and anger.

Consequently, after twelve years of marriage, I became a single mother of four children. We lived 1,500 miles away from family and friends, so not only was I without a support system, I had no Plan B. It was a risky move to transition four children (including an infant and a special needs child) into a home with only one income. Certainly I had fears; I wondered if I would be able to financially support four children on my own.

Would I hit a roadblock and have to return to my unhealthy situation to afford the cost of living? How would I balance maintaining a career with the demands of a special needs child, doctor visits, sick children, early pick-ups, and mishaps at school? And when would I have time for myself?

When I began planning my departure, I connected with organizations like *The Family Place* and *Hope's Door*. Both of these specific organizations helped me leave my unhealthy living situation. I was humbled by the amount of support I received from family, friends, and local organizations. Through the favor of God and the help of those He touched, I was able to obtain a new place of employment, new residence, vehicle, and many other resources. Essentially, I had transitioned to a new life.

During this time God continued to reassure me that I was not forgotten. I nearly lost myself in the twelve years I spent pouring into and sacrificing everything for my marriage, which I still don't regret doing. But it was liberating when God spoke those words to me: "You are not forgotten." From then on I could feel Him reviving my dreams, hopes, ambitions, and goals. He began tearing down negative thoughts and replacing them with His truth about who I was in *His* eyes. I could *feel* that I was not forgotten and that God had a plan for me, even though my life was less than perfect.

Freedom began the day I realized God was in the midst of my imperfect life and that He loves me and has a plan for me, even while I'm in the process of becoming something better. I no longer wait for my "perfect plans" to unfold, nor do I let my adversities define who I am or influence how I think God views me. I know God is with me, and, most importantly, I know what He thinks of me. I am the apple of His eye *today* and He longs to be with me *today*. So when I feel like I'm twelve years behind schedule, I lift my eyes up to the hills and remember that I am exactly where I need to be. No person or mistake can change the plans that God has for me.

Today, I still face adversity but I have accomplished more goals in the last two years than I did when I was in my unhealthy marital situation with two incomes and the additional help. I have been able to redevelop my business as a jewelry designer and start my home business as a virtual assistant offering administrative assistance to small business owners on a project basis. Having this freedom has allowed me to be available to my children throughout the day. I have been able to focus on growth and healing (for myself and for my children), restore my financial history, return to school, and so much more. I am now connected with support groups, such as an adult Bible fellowship through my church and Celebrate Recovery®, an amazing Christ-centered program that helps people "overcome their hurts, hang-ups, and habits."

Although my story is still in the developing stages, I feel tremendously blessed to have the opportunity to rebuild my life and provide my children with a safe and healthy environment. I am overwhelmed by the support and grace God has given me to grow. It is only by God's goodness that I am who I am today.

Whatever season of life you are in, love *today*! Love yourself today; love your family today; love your friends today. Meanwhile, embrace the adversities in life, knowing that God is taking you *through* them and you are right where you need to be.

Sherri's Tips:
Better or Bitter—The Choice is Yours!

What is forgiveness? Generally, forgiveness is a decision to let go of resentment and thoughts of revenge. The act that hurt or offended you may always remain a part of your life, but forgiveness can lessen its grip on you and help you focus on the positive parts of your life. Forgiveness can even lead to feelings of understanding, empathy, and compassion for the one who hurt you.

Forgiveness doesn't mean that you deny the other person's responsibility for hurting you, and it doesn't minimize or justify the wrong. You can forgive the person without excusing the act. Forgiveness brings a kind of peace that helps you go on with life.

What are the benefits of forgiving someone? Letting go of grudges and bitterness makes way for compassion, kindness, and peace. Forgiveness can lead to:
- healthier relationships;
- greater spiritual and psychological well-being;
- less stress and hostility;
- lower blood pressure;
- fewer symptoms of depression, anxiety, and chronic pain; and
- lower risk of alcohol and substance abuse.

Why is it so easy to hold a grudge? When you have been hurt by someone you love and trust, you may become angry, sad, or confused. If you dwell on hurtful events or situations, grudges filled with resentment, vengeance, and hostility may take root. If you allow negative feelings to crowd out positive feelings, you may find yourself swallowed up by your own bitterness or sense of injustice.

What are the effects of holding a grudge? If you're unforgiving, you may pay the price repeatedly by bringing anger and bitterness into every relationship and new experience. Your life may become so wrapped up in the wrong that you can't enjoy the present. You may become depressed or anxious. You may feel your life lacks meaning or purpose, or that you're at odds with your spiritual beliefs. You may lose valuable and enriching connectedness with others.

How do I reach a state of forgiveness? Forgiveness is a commitment to a process of change. The first step is to recognize the value of forgiveness and its importance in your life at a given time. Then reflect on the facts of the situation: how you've reacted and how this combination has affected your life, health, and well-being. When you're ready, actively choose to forgive the person who's offended you. Move away from your role as victim and release the control and power the offending person and situation has had in your life. As you let go of grudges, you'll no longer define your life by how you've been hurt. You may even find compassion and understanding.

"Cast your cares on the Lord and he will
sustain you; he will never let the righteous fall"
—Psalm 55:22 NIV

11

Overcoming Adversity

"It's only when we run into ourselves that we can
reach outside of ourselves for help."
—Kristina Wandzilak

*There are things that happen in life that you simply don't have the business
plan to handle. What do you do when you're faced with life's biggest
challenges, such as breast cancer, the loss of a job, or another serious hurdle?
My personal advice to the women I coach is to be prepared for life events we
can do something about, like the three Ds (death, divorce, and disability).
It's said that whatever you overcome makes you stronger. That's certainly true
for the women included in this book.*

Sherri Elliott-Yeary

Every day thousands of thoughts come to our minds; some are
good and some are bad. But for us to be positive and healthy

women, we must focus on the good thoughts and let go of the bad. Yet it's always such a temptation to hold on to the bad thoughts. Our minds have had so much practice operating freely that it seems we don't have to use much effort at all to think wrong or negative thoughts. The effort comes in learning to think positively.

Positive minds produce positive lives, but the opposite is also true. It can be very difficult to switch your way of thinking. Some women are afraid to hope because they have been hurt so much in life. They have had disappointments, and they don't think they can face the pain of another letdown.

Battles are fought in our minds every day. When we begin to feel the battle of the mind is just too difficult and we are about to give up, that's when we must choose to resist negative thoughts and determine we are going to rise above our problems and succeed.

When I was twelve years old, Cathy Reid, a member of the Big Sister organization, and her wonderful parents, Marj and Les Ford, took me into their home and adopted me. They saw something in me I was not able to see: that I was worth something. The members of the Ford family shared their lives with me, treating me like their sister and daughter. Marj and Les were in their fifties, and all of their kids were grown and out of the house. What possessed them to take on a troubled twelve-year-old girl?

If Marj were alive today, I would ask her that question, but she passed away when I was in my early twenties from a long and difficult disease. The Ford family loved me, supported me, and showed me what a real family is. This was the first time in my life I felt loved, protected, and safe. I am eternally grateful to all of them for the important part they had in making me the woman I am today.

When I was twelve years old, Marj gave me sage advice: "When you're handed lemons, make lemonade." That old adage has helped me handle many challenges in life with strength and optimism.

As I started planning this book, I reflected on all of the lessons I learned from my brief time in the Ford family. It was apparent to me that no matter how difficult the challenge, Marj and Les took it on and displayed love and acceptance.

During a call with a potential contributor for the book, I asked if she had her contribution ready and she replied, "No, I'm having a hard time writing because I still feel like I'm in the trenches." My response was, "Aren't we all!"

I believe we are all in the trenches in some way—with relationships, health issues, career problems, etc. What matters most during those times is to be mindful and appreciative of the gifts and blessing we have in our lives, not just the place where we are "stuck."

Despite all the blessings in my life, I'm in a trench right now, which proves the point of this book. I have it all in so many ways, but there's something I can't have right now.

As a result of a surgery last year, my lymphatic system has been damaged. Twice a day, every day, I have to be connected to a lymphedema machine for sixty minutes of lymphatic drainage massage to increase my lymph circulation. Taking the time and energy to heal my body has altered my normally very active lifestyle. I can no longer engage in any activity that could harm my lymph system, as it causes swelling. That means rollerblading lessons are out for a while!

As part of accepting this new challenge, I need to embrace the changes that are required of me if I'm going to live a "normal" life. However, in Texas, we have summer weather eight months a year and I have to be careful in the sun and limit my time in the pool or a hot bath.

One beautiful Saturday afternoon, I was feeling particularly low and sorry for myself when my husband asked me an important question. He asked, "If the doctor told you last year there was a slight chance as a result of surgery you might get lymphedema, would that have changed your mind?" I said, "No, it wouldn't have. I don't believe in the odds; if I did, I would not be where I am today in other areas of my life."

Mason had a very valid point. I decided to turn this daily obstacle into an opportunity to enjoy quiet time with a good book or television show that I might not allow myself otherwise.

Mary Golaboff
Human Resources Consultant

When I graduated from Texas A&M University at age twenty-seven, my written goal was to be a vice president of a company by age thirty-five. At age thirty-two, I reached my goal as VP of human resources.

I worked long hours, traveled, and met and worked with people that are still in my circle of friends. All the feedback I received was terrific. The company put all of its management team through intense leadership development programs, and I benefited greatly. All was right with the world, and my career was on the trajectory I had always envisioned.

Fast forward: new company, high profile position. I was asked to leave after two years of blood, sweat, and tears. My high-flying career had just been annihilated with the wave of the hand of someone who did not fully appreciate my efforts.

The mental devastation of being asked to leave a company by the owner, whose vision I wholeheartedly believed in, left me in shambles. So I asked myself, "What were my mistakes? How can I put myself back together?"

Although a part of me wanted to rehash the events and talk to my previous employer, I knew it would be a waste of time and energy. I've heard that success is the best revenge, but I believe that is incorrect. Revenge is pointless and creates a negative aura. Instead, grab on to who you are and focus on what you love as the catalyst to propel you forward.

I recovered professionally but soon had to face a personal challenge. My doctor informed me I had cancer. Then I lost my composure.

I kept wondering how this could happen to me. I thought, *I take care of myself, I work out, I eat well most of the time, I get plenty of rest, I don't smoke, I barely drink alcohol, and now I have cancer.*

How am I going to work to support myself and those I love? How am I going to tell my parents? What is this type of cancer and how can I fight it?

I called my two sisters and my two closest friends and cried with them. I knew I could not tell my elderly parents over the phone, so I didn't. I only told them the doctor wanted to take my thyroid out, but I did not share the cancer piece until later.

Prior to the surgery, I allowed myself to grieve. I felt as though a fog had descended and parked right in the middle of my life. The sobs came in two distinct categories: the body wracking type, which could be defined as hysterical, and the quiet sobs that seemed to last forever.

When I arrived at my surgeon's office, I was nervous to hear what he would say. I was hungry for information about my cancer. My two closest friends were with me, armed with questions and timelines. We were all on edge, but once my surgeon outlined the procedure and gave me statistics on survival rates, I started to believe I could beat this!

Getting the information from my surgeon was absolutely reassuring. Now I needed to share this information with those closest to me, as I knew my cancer would rock their worlds. My priorities shifted as I started to see the impact this was having on my perspectives and the perspectives of those around me. I experienced a reorganization of what is important to me. This journey took me to a new level and required me to reexamine my priorities. What I clearly experienced is that everyone deals with situations differently based on their information, how they accept it, and how they deal with their own fear. They acknowledge the reality of the situation with varying degrees of acceptance.

My priorities have shifted in subtle ways. I am more conscientious of my time and how I spend it. Changing my priorities strengthened my personal and professional relationships, clarified my consistency on exercising and good eating habits, and propelled me to try new experiences with less fear. I appreciate that behaviors are based on the information people have at the time, so I've learned to ask more questions. I'm more forgiving of myself and others.

My journey continues.

Dr. Venus Opal Reese

Personal and Professional Development Expert

When I was sixteen years old, I was living on the streets of Baltimore, Maryland. There were drugs, prostitutes, and police all around me. The stench of stale beer and urine on the sidewalk was right beside me like an unwanted companion wrapping its arms around me, and I asked myself, "How did I get here? And how do I get out?"

My birth mother, whom I call Mama, had put me out on the street, and this was not the first time. I slept on park benches, in strangers' houses, and at bus stations, and I got my meals from churches.

Throughout all this I still went to school, but the students poked fun at me and the teachers pretended they did not notice my situation. Except for one.

Mrs. Judy Francis, my ninth grade math teacher, took time to take care of me. She helped me to get cleaned up, got me a warm meal, and dropped me off at the street corner and never asked me questions or insisted that I explain myself. She didn't judge. I could keep my dignity. It was a big deal to me not to have to defend myself or blame others.

That was the basis of my transformation. I started to stay after school to help her, and she would always feed me and take me where I wanted to go. There was a period where I didn't talk at all because it hurt too much. Mrs. Francis said, "If you're not going to talk, then write!" She gave me a pencil and pad, and she spoke with such conviction that I figured I should follow her advice.

My thoughts came out as poetry. Mrs. Francis read them, typed them, and sent them off to the NAACP ACT-SO competition. I won in the poetry category.

Mrs. Francis gave me the tools to have a voice and took unsolicited action on my behalf. She gave it to me for free, and I was accustomed to having to trade. On the streets, nothing is free. When she looked at me, she saw somebody who mattered: someone worth her time, money, and attention. That thought was like a door with creaking hinges; the idea that my life didn't have to look like my circumstances was new to me. It was a profound change.

She said, "Venus, you should go to college." I thought, *Are you crazy?* No one in my immediate family had graduated from high school for generations. Besides, I didn't know how to spell. Yet, fourteen years later, to everyone's amazement, I graduated from Stanford University with a second master's degree and a PhD. The moment I sent off the last chapter of my dissertation, I realized it was time for me to do the impossible: call Mama.

I wanted Mrs. Francis, whom I called Nanna, and Mama to walk me across the stage at graduation. I wanted Mama to know she mattered and was loved. They both came and walked me across that graduation stage. I granted my mother grace and learned it's not always about overcoming; sometimes it's about letting go. Sometimes you have to let go of your own point of view. I learned that setting others straight might cost too much. I may win the battle, but not the war.

You may have to let go of something to overcome adversity. But when you let go, you soar.

What comes up is pure joy.

Cindy Colangelo

Offers Consulting Services For Nonprofit Organizations

The first time the doctors found cancer in me, I was forty-two. My doctor found a lump during my annual visit that was later confirmed with a mammogram. I had a lumpectomy, followed by six weeks of radiation.

The second time, I was diagnosed through a breast exam. I was fifty-one. Despite going through a double mastectomy, six rounds of chemo, and six weeks of radiation, I hadn't even been through with treatment for a year when I found another lump.

It was New Year's Eve, and I was getting dressed to go out. You could see it, a lump in the reconstructed breast in the little bit of breast tissue that had remained.

If you remove the breasts, you think you're safe; that's not always true. I have a type of cancer that is very aggressive; but on a positive note, there is a drug that is very effective against it.

Now I'm in a clinical trial study for stage 4 metastatic breast cancer. Hopefully the drug and treatment will be approved as one of the new standards of care in the near future. I've been experiencing great results, and the side effects are minimal—I've been able to keep my hair, maintain my appetite, and have not experienced any nausea.

As one of the only participants in this study in Dallas, I feel blessed to be able to be on the cutting edge of this therapy. My guardian angel has been working overtime, and everything that could go right seems to have gone that way. The study lasts for five and a half years. Every three weeks, I go for a two-hour infusion.

My family, friends, and faith are helping me do this. My husband and I are Catholic, and we practice our faith now more than ever. As much as I can, I give myself positive messaging through spiritual and motivational reading.

If I can leave you with one message, it's this: Don't hide your head in the sand; know what you are facing. You must have good information. Things change quickly so you have to be an active participant in your own care; don't wait for someone else to do it for you.

It's a daily up and down. I don't always have energy. I give myself permission to take days slowly. No one can give 100 percent 100 percent of the time. We expect so much, and put so much pressure on ourselves, that we often compound the problems we have. We need to give ourselves permission to rebalance, step out of the fast lane, and not feel guilty for doing a little less.

There's always hope. You hear about outcomes that are unexpected. It happens. So don't ever give up.

Sherri's Tips:
Overcoming Adversity

You have to overcome many obstacles to be successful. This is true no matter what endeavor you are pursuing. If you are working on a big goal, I guarantee you there are going to be problems, issues, and roadblocks along the way.

This is not negative, it is reality. Accept it and prepare yourself to overcome the obstacles. Don't fret about it; just get ready to handle it quickly and decisively. The issue you encounter could be in the form of a technical problem, or it could be someone who doesn't see eye to eye with you. Either way, you have to successfully overcome obstacles if you want to achieve your goals. Here is how I deal with obstacles when they arise in my life:

- **Troubleshoot and diagnose the root cause.** The quickest way to solve any problem is to find its root cause. What is at the very source of the issue? It usually takes some time to determine this. However, the time is well spent because once you know the root cause, you can address it and move on. People often oppose you out of fear. You need to determine exactly what it is about the action you are taking that makes them afraid and address it with them. Here's a hint: it usually isn't the first thing they tell you.

- **Listen to your gut instinct.** I can't count the times I solved problems by simply following my gut. For me, this is the nagging little idea in the back of my head that doesn't really seem logical, but ends up being the solution anyway. In almost every case, I try to dismiss it by reasoning it couldn't possibly be the right thing to try. However, once I give in, I find it leads me to exactly the solution I desired. Listen to your gut. It often knows what to do.

- **Research the problem online.** Generally, if you are faced with overcoming an obstacle to achieve your goal, someone else has already encountered it and solved it. Don't reinvent the wheel; just find out what others have done and apply their experiences to your situation. This is one of the fabulous things about the Internet. It is a huge archive of ideas for solving almost any imaginable problem. I love using Google to help find solutions to all kinds of issues. In addition, you might try my blog, www.RealWomenHavingItAll.com, or my website, www.GenerationalGuru.com, to find top quality articles pertaining to personal development, finances, entrepreneurship, and many other similar topics.

- **Recruit the assistance of others.** Get your friends, family, and coworkers involved to help think of ways to overcome the obstacle. Remember, two heads are better than one. Often these people will have different perspectives on the situation that can lead to an immediate breakthrough. Also, they can serve as champions or cheerleaders to help move you past the challenge you are facing.

- **Hire an expert.** Sometimes you need to call in the big guns. If the problem is in an area outside your expertise and is particularly nasty, then you should probably bring in an expert. Make sure your expert has successfully dealt with similar dilemmas in the past. Ask for references, and call them to confirm the situation was similar and the resolution was complete. Document the obstacle and the exact outcome you expect in writing. You and the expert should both sign this agreement *before* any work is done.

- **Change *your* attitude toward the situation.** Sometimes *we* are the problem. Evaluate your attitudes to see if a change in the way you are looking at the situation might help to overcome the problem. This is especially useful in situations where the obstacle is another person. You might need to change your attitude toward this person in order to gain his or her cooperation. It is going to take some maturity, but the results are often astonishing.

- **Use trial and error.** When all else fails or when your situation is unique, you may need to experiment. Obviously this isn't the most efficient way to overcome an obstacle, but it may be your only option. Be as scientific in your approach as possible. Go slowly and evaluate each of your trial solutions as carefully as possible. Sometimes it takes a combination of solutions to achieve the best results.

- **Sleep on it.** I have had numerous stubborn problems where I spent hours trying to solve them with no success. Then I gave up, went to bed, and awoke the next morning with a new idea that fixed the situation almost immediately. Sometimes we just need to give our brains some time to rest and work on the issue. It is often hard to walk away, but sometimes this is the best thing to do.

- **Never give up.** Don't quit! I am reminded of a quote from Vince Lombardi: "Winners never quit, and quitters never win." This is so true! You may have to back up, turn around, or take a completely different approach, but you can never stop trying to get past the present roadblock. Perseverance is what will lead to success. I refer to people that attack problems with the same level of tenacity as bulldogs. They persist until they find a solution no matter what odds are against them. This is the only path to success!

- **Start over.** When all else fails, start over at the beginning. Maybe one of your foundational assumptions about the issue is wrong. Reevaluate everything. If you are having this much trouble, then it is likely you haven't identified the root cause or have framed the issue incorrectly. Make sure you understand the problem clearly and completely to get it resolved quickly.

Overcoming adversity is critical to success. Almost every goal you pursue will have its obstacles. If you want to succeed, you must master the art of problem solving. These tips will send you in the right direction. Move past the hurdles quickly to cross the finish line to victory!

"For every child of God defeats this evil world, and we achieve this victory through our faith."
—*1 John 5:4* NLT

12

You Are Who
You Are
Supposed To Be

"Without dreams, the poet has no rhyme, the musician
has no song, and the artist no beauty."
—Anonymous

*It's great to be you. It's not so great to try to be someone you're not. One of
the greatest challenges of growing up is deciding who you want to be. As you
try on costumes in your mind, you might not know right away which one fits
the best.*

Sherri Elliott-Yeary

Have you ever wondered what makes an extraordinary person?
An extraordinary person is an ordinary person who makes extraordinary choices. Extraordinary people hold bigger visions for
themselves than the ones dictated by their underlying commitments. They allow their individual lives to be used to serve the

world around them. Extraordinary people make choices that are consistent not only with the highest expression of themselves but with the greater good of the world. If you closely examine people you consider to be extraordinary, you will find they are committed to excellence, making a contribution, not settling, setting an example for others, and living the life they are meant to live. Each of us has extraordinary potential. The promise of a flower lives within every seed, and within each of us lies the ability to lead an extraordinary life.

When, as a young child, I saw all of the kids in the nice houses my school bus drove passed on our route, I knew I wanted to do whatever their dad did when I grew up. I had no idea that women worked too; I only knew I had no dad and that was why we did not live like the rest of the kids at school. I know I have a choice to either allow myself to mourn my lost childhood or understand how it helped shape me into the woman, wife, and mother I am today.

It used to be that choosing a profession was easy. Women went eagerly into nursing, teaching, and administration; there were not as many choices then. Not many girls dreamed of taking companies public or helping to rule a nation. Women learned later that we had many more opportunities available to us in the business world. Learning to be CEOs and division leaders while our children went to day care was a challenge yet to be faced.

Maybe you decided to be a teacher. That's great! You have the ability to impact thousands of lives. You're surrounded by eager-to-learn students, beaming with love and admiration for you. Underneath your prim button-down blouse, there's an S on your chest. You're a "Super Teacher," saving our children from illiteracy! You may laugh, but if you don't, who will? You could be the one person who finds a better way of doing things, no matter what you do for a living. You may pioneer a better way to teach children that every public school in the nation will adopt. You could be the researcher who finds the cure for AIDS or the politician who brings jobs back to America.

But what if you're not the heroic type? You can make a great difference for many people simply by being the best you that you can be. In today's high-pressure, morally confused culture, that alone is pretty heroic.

As your best self, you are able to reduce the complications in your life. You can choose to set a wonderful example for generations to follow. No matter what you do, what you leave behind is a foundation and legacy that can be built upon by the next person. You may not find the cure for AIDS, but your work can offer clues to the next researcher until a cure is found. You may not single-handedly restore the American economy, but you can be the entrepreneur that brings employment to at least one person—*yourself!*

Few people give much thought to greatness, because it's simply not in most of us. What we don't realize is that even the smallest acts of generosity, courage, empathy, and faith have value. All of our lives, no matter how big or small, have value because we have the ability to influence the greater good to be even better.

Sometimes we choose who we want to be when we grow up; sometimes we get direction from God or others. But only we can choose to be our best self and show up by living the life we were meant to live.

Showing up today and paying the price today determines tomorrow's success. If you want a guarantee, forget it. Trust your vision and gut instincts and eventually the joy of success will be yours.

As you think about who you are supposed to be, you might consider that you did not get to this place right now without experiencing a few failures and mistakes. Mistakes are how you learn what you want in life and how to hone the skills necessary to achieve the life you want and to be the woman you are supposed to be.

A close friend of mine, Karen Hunt, who works for a drug and alcohol rehabilitation facility, took my daughter Khirsten and me on a tour of their new facility. When we finished, Khirsten looked at me and said, "Mom, I wish this incredible place of peace and healing had been here when I needed help." I knew in that moment I was in the right place at the right time to experience this blessing with my friend Karen and my daughter Khirsten, who had just celebrated her four-year anniversary being clean from drug abuse. I paused for a moment to silently give God thanks for people like Karen and the exceptional treatment facilities available to families dealing with addiction when they need help the most. After our tour, Karen presented both of us with a polished stone, which I now carry in my handbag. It reminds me to focus on the moment and opportunity to make a difference for others in times of uncertainty.

One of my favorite quotes by Mahatma Gandhi perfectly captures what I'm trying to share with you: *"You must be the change you want to see in the world."*

Blanche Evans

Award-Winning Writer and Oil Painter

If you look back over your life, there is probably a defining moment you can point to and say, "That's who I am." For me, that moment was when I decided I could fly.

It was 1960. *Peter Pan* was on television, and it was my turn to have the top bunk bed while my twin sister took the bottom. Our mother pioneered the use of the television as a babysitter and cleverly installed one in our bedroom. We watched the show with fascination, delighting in Tinkerbell, a small, flickering light fairy who dispensed fairy dust and lots of attitude as she jealously guarded Peter Pan. We were awed by the notion of a flying buccaneer's galleon and cheered Peter Pan's triumph over Captain Hook and the pirates.

When the show was over, I was too excited to go to sleep. I kept replaying the story over and over in my mind. I didn't understand how television worked or that Peter Pan was really an Emmy-winning actress named Mary Martin, not a lost little boy at all. I just remembered what Peter told the Darling children: if you wanted to fly, all you had to do was *believe*. At age seven, I was probably old enough to know better, but my imagination kicked caution aside. I whipped myself up into a fearless certainty that I could fly too, right through the window and off to Neverland!

So I got out of the covers, stood at the edge of the top bunk, squeezed my eyes shut, shouted "Believe!" and took the proverbial leap of faith. I flapped my arms all the way down as I crashed right into the linoleum floor. As I lay there, shocked, bruised, and bleeding, my twin—ever the wiser one—rolled on her side and wryly observed, "You idiot . . . you didn't have any fairy dust."

The humiliation was worse than having my chin stitched up by the doctor. How could I have been so stupid? To crash and burn in front of my smarty-pants twin was too much to bear. However, I was soon over it, and the memory of that night did little to discourage me from being who I really am: a risk taker. That's in my nature, just like it's my twin's nature to be cautious. Maybe she's watched me take it on the chin one too many times, but I'm happy to report that she's also seen me soar.

To this day, I'm glad I tried to fly, if for no other reason than having a funny story to tell. But I did learn something valuable: Next time, be prepared. If you believe you can fly, make sure you have plenty of fairy dust. Check to make sure the window is open. Night air can be chilly, so bring a sweater. And, just in case, it won't hurt to drag your mattress onto the floor.

Sarah Spence
Human Resource Professional

I believe Sherri saw potential in me and knew I needed a nudge in the right direction. I met Sherri through my last employer at a construction company. I had two years of human resources experience when I took the position of HR manager. Sherri mentored me during this time and encouraged me to develop my career at a more sophisticated company that had the resources to provide the support I needed to develop my skills and knowledge. She provided me with a lead to a prestigious skin care and cosmetics manufacturer. I had to check my ego at the door and accept an entry-level position because Sherri made me realize that, with only two years of experience, I had not really earned the senior title I held at my previous job.

That taught me an important lesson: do not turn down a good opportunity just because of your ego. I am glad I was able to understand and recognize that in order to move up the corporate ladder (or lattice) with a better company, I had to leave the fancy title behind to grow and develop in my chosen field.

Everyone has something they can teach you. Every relationship you build is worth your time, as Sherri demonstrated to me.

Michele Benjamin
Regional Sales Manager for a Technology Firm

Living alone seemed to suit me well. I was making good money and had built my first home. During a business trip, I met Terry, a retired police officer. We knew right away we had something special. In less than a year, Terry relocated to Texas to be near me so we could start dating.

I was thirty-eight when we married; I had chosen to delay marriage until after I "did it all."

Terry completely changed my life, exposing me to the idea that marriage wasn't the end of my life, but a great new beginning. We're so much alike, with our interest in aviation in particular. He's taught me about guns, and we love discussing politics. Without him, I would never have had the courage and strength

to do what was right for my niece, Nicole.

Nicole, a little white-haired angel, was born to my brother and his girl-friend. I made it a point to be a part of Nicole's life. Her parents seem to be focused on them-selves instead of her. Terry and I decided to start visiting her more often.

It became clear that she needed someone to take care of her full-time. We took her in because it was the right thing to do for a child in need, and we just recently completed her formal adoption. It was the greatest gift and blessing we could have ever been given.

Then came September 11, 2001.

It caused great confusion in our country and made companies more cautious in their decisions, affecting my job. As adults, Terry and I were able to try to put the event in perspective, but Nicole was at the age where she wondered if these kinds of things happened all the time. It took a long time of reassuring her before she felt confident that planes didn't normally fly into buildings.

During this period, it was a struggle to balance my life. My health became a factor because of a back injury. I wasn't able to exercise, so I gained weight, further exacerbating the challenges in my life. Once I realized that one of the benefits of marriage was that I didn't have to do everything myself, I realized what a gift my new husband was. While it was hard to let go of some responsibilities at first, I found Terry a reliable and willing participant, especially with Nicole. He was able to remove the emotions I was feeling toward my brother in the decisions we had to make, and he helped to put what was best for Nicole in perspective.

All of this came together in just a matter of months. I quickly learned I can take on more than I had ever imagined. I learned I could rely on others. I still make mistakes, but I get through them because I am supported by my family and my faith in God.

Sherri's Tips: Become Your Best Self

I believe we are each on a personal journey filled with challenges and opportunities; we are seeking connection with our mental, physical, and spiritual realms of life. We often look for answers, but sometimes they don't come as quickly as we want. We become impatient, discouraged, frustrated, angry, and stuck. Instead, we need to be mindful and patient. Life is not a race, but a tour to be appreciated and savored each step of the way.

Take the time to dream, nourishing your body, mind, and spirit. Breathe deeply and enjoy the boundless blessings you have today. To become your best self, try the following:

- **Develop relationships with highly creative people.** Creative people see opportunity everywhere and their insight will rub off on you. The best way to learn to see a world of possibilities is to hang out with people that spend most of their time actively creating things. There are amazing possibilities in this, as there are endless opportunities that connectedness provides.

- **Write down everything that surprises you.** Many great opportunities are fueled by surprises, and they are usually funny, amazing, and insightful. Carry a small notebook in your purse and note everything that surprises you. You will find the opportunity to create new ideas from what you notice in life as surprises.

- **Journal about problems.** Some people say there is no such thing as a problem; there are only opportunities. I concede they may be right. For every problem there is a solution, and that solution will have value to others. Documenting obstacles, problems, and the solutions you use to overcome them is an opportunity for you to bring value to others.

- **Journal about possibilities.** Imagine grand possibilities and write them down. Imagine the life you want to live. What would it look like? How would we use it? Imagine yourself being the greatest possible person you can be. What would you be? Imagine your dream business. Imagine the future you would create if you could create any possible future. Find the opportunities hidden inside your imagination.

- **Be open to unorthodox ideas.** If your first reaction to an idea is defensive, stop yourself—think, wait, listen, and let the person finish explaining. Listen to the entire idea and then imagine the possibility of the idea. Don't shoot down an idea just because it sounds strange. Give it a moment, wait for your defensiveness to pass, and then look at it again. Sleep on it or wait several days to get your prejudices out of the way. It has taken years of persistence for me to accept several unorthodox ideas that have proven very valuable.

- **Eliminate limiting beliefs and mind-sets.** Are you one of those people who says, "I'm just not that creative"? Are you willing to indulge your curiosity or are you afraid of looking foolish? Do you feel a need to follow the rules without question? All of these things come from limiting beliefs and mind-sets that will restrict your ability to see opportunities available to you. Identify and smash your limiting beliefs.

- **Be grateful.** Be grateful for your gifts *and* your weaknesses. Be grateful for your successes *and* your setbacks. If you are grateful for all things, including those that challenge you, you will be able to see them as the opportunities they are.

*"But our bodies have many parts, and God has
put each part just where he wants it"*
—*I Corinthians 12:18* NLT

13

Authentic Leadership

"Get comfortable with being uncomfortable."
—Sherri Elliott-Yeary

In business, we grow or we die. Most of us are willing to stretch when it comes to our careers. It's expected. You strive for a bigger paycheck, a bigger office, more influence, or more power. Why don't we do the same in our personal lives? One naturally affects the other. In life, as in business, when we neglect growth, the passion inside you cools. It is important not only to plan and save for the new house or car but also to invest in our inner growth. As we grow older we shed the previous version of ourselves as we each create the new person we are today by embarking on a lifetime of learning.

Sherri Elliott-Yeary

I recently saw a friend at the grocery store and I could tell she really wanted to stop and chat. However, I had more than sixty

women coming to my home for a quarterly "Wine & Women" event and had not had time to adequately prepare. I had to quickly explain that I couldn't talk right then because I had to go home to prepare.

Later that evening, I felt a prompting in my heart that my friend may have misunderstood. I called to let her know I was sorry I couldn't visit, explaining that I had to be home to prepare for my guests. Years ago I wouldn't have done that. I would have taken the attitude, "If she was offended, that is her problem." But I've learned I want to be a woman of God who walks the talk and acts like an authentic leader, not the kind of woman that other women talk about. I genuinely try to walk in love and strive not to offend anyone if I can possibly avoid it.

I wonder how often we have considered a person to be an enemy simply because she spoke some truth we did not want to hear. She might have been a great friend. I am sure that the spirit of offense is a tremendous thief of good friendships. When we ask a question, many of us really don't want the truth. We want people to tell us what we want to hear.

Become known as a woman of God who walks the talk as an authentic leader that Jesus has laid out for every one of us.

In today's fast-paced world, we must continuously strive for knowledge. In fact, it's predicted that the wealthy people of the current and future decades will be the owners of knowledge and information. I try to learn something new every day by opening a book or watching a documentary.

Start a study group of other lifetime leaders like I did. We call ourselves the Passionate Organization of Women, or POW for short. Our group consists of thought leaders ranging in age from twenty-eight to sixty-eight, all from different professions. Collectively, we are now stronger and more permanent because of our alliance. We are women, and, while we can do anything alone, we are magnificent together.

You don't want to wake up five years from now and greet the same person in the mirror. You want to see a woman who has transcended her former boundaries and grown in her capability to lead others.

Smart women appreciate that what works today won't necessarily work tomorrow and understand that aggressive learning is a competitive advantage to achieving any desired goals. Every busy schedule has at least one daily ten-minute opportunity to feed the leader within you.

To me, what makes a great leader is integrity, and women prove every day that they have what it takes. According to a New Jersey polling group, the most trusted profession is nursing. Ninety-four percent of nurses are women. Conversely, women make up less than seven percent of the prison population, which tells us, on the whole, women can be trusted to abide by laws and do the right thing. I cannot believe this powerful set of facts is accidental.

A Chinese proverb says, "If you stand straight do not fear a crooked shadow." Perhaps women stand straighter than men because we're more emotionally analytical. The emotional "why" tugs at us, and, based on our interpretation of cause and effect, we form opinions on how to act. Our interpretations feed our integrity.

Integrity has the final say in whether we will rise or decline, be whole or broken. When uncompromising integrity is our guide, success is authentic. And the joy of success is authentic. No one can take that success away from you when it is accomplished by living intentionally with integrity.

Integrity is a way of living in which mind, body, and spirit unite consistently. When any part of your life is out of congruence with other parts, you can feel incomplete and out of sorts. I know I do. Integrity is the strength that makes you whole.

Temptations abound in the business world, as they do in our personal environment. No matter how complex a decision appears on the surface, when stripped down to the basics, it's usually plain and simple: Do what's right, not what's most appealing. That's what we need of our leaders today.

Petey Parker
Leadership Consultant,
Keynote Speaker, and Entrepreneur

To lead or not to lead? If that is the question, then perhaps it's time to define what a leader is.

John Quincy Adams once said, "If your actions inspire others to dream more, learn more, do more, become more, you are a leader."

As I think about the people and events in my life that have influenced me, it's quite clear that any of my perceived success has been accomplished through the grace of a higher power. It's necessary to be led and learn to follow before you find yourself worthy of calling yourself a leader.

It's interesting how much our past plays a part in our future. Like many others, my goal was to rise above my circumstances and lead the life I was meant to lead. I had to learn to choose to be positive instead of negative to make wonderful, glorious things happen for myself and others.

I was raised by my grandmother and my mom, who was a single working mother. This was back when single mothers were very uncommon. My father walked out on us after taking the few pennies I had saved out of my piggy bank. We were so poor my clothes were made from flour sacks, and my classmates at school made fun of me and threw stones at me.

It hurt, but Mom taught me that being creative made up for being poor and that the ability to smile and laugh in the face of negativity was a rare but achievable trait.

I got lost in fantasy by lining up my stuffed bears as a captive audience and entertaining them with funny stories and positive endings. They were my first nonpaying audience, and their silent enthrallment with my performance helped me gain the confidence I needed to inspire thousands through paid speaking engagements and boardroom-level consulting, which happened much later in my life.

- *I dreamed* as an escape from the reality of being so poor and the awareness of all the sacrifices being made by Grandma and Mom to hold us together.
- *I learned* from my grandmother not to sit in judgment of anyone's beliefs.
- *I did more* to help by making creative potholders and selling them door to door to contribute to our funds.

- *And I learned* to become more understanding and respectful and to find the "happy" within challenging situations.

I didn't know it, but I was learning to become a leader. Leadership began for me when I chose not to accept negative surroundings and, instead, to keep a positive vision in front of myself. As a young adult, I couldn't wait to reach out to the world. I dreamed about becoming a flight attendant where I could see the world and meet exciting people. In working with the public as a flight attendant, I witnessed the best and worst of humanity. People usually try to do the best they can, but I grew less and less tolerant of people who kept themselves and others from becoming all they could be. I decided to discover the uniqueness in people and played to their strengths by trying to imagine walking in their shoes.

Like lots of young women, I made some poor choices and had to make a concerted effort to own up to my mistakes. While living life a little too frivolously, I could only dream of having an impressive and well-earned career, of holding a position that would make a difference in the community, and of having an income that would provide luxury and peace of mind.

One day, I decided to do something about it, but I went too far in the other direction and became a slave to money, working in overdrive. I added aggressiveness and obsession to my behavior, all of which have absolutely nothing to do with being a good leader, unless used for lessons learned. I realized motivation creates behavior, and behavior creates consequences.

Being capable of affording luxury does not buy peace of mind, or good mental or physical health. The communities we serve start at home, and it's imperative to know who you are, where you are, and why you're there at any given time.

You really only have two choices when it comes to a challenging situation. You either learn to live with it or do something to

172

change it. There is nothing in-between.

So, as the next step, I created a positive vision of my own future and did something about making it a reality. I resigned from a prestigious C-level career. I was blessed to find and marry into a wonderful family who gave me incredible support and the sense of belonging that only family and friends can give. I surrounded myself with entrepreneurs who helped me develop a new understanding and appreciation for having the courage to run a business the way it should be done.

They taught me the difference between leadership, management, sales, administration, and the resources available for creating more productive accomplishments. They instilled the importance of beginning with a firm foundation built on standards and never letting go of the basics or the loyalty of those folks giving guidance (sometimes negative and sometimes positive, but always in an effort to make you better.)

I became more knowledgeable about the gaps in everyday business and what can be done to handle generational and gender differences, communication, business planning, aligning mission statements with goals, and other disconnects between what needs to be done and what is actually implemented.

This knowledge became the foundation for my consulting business, and I am grateful to anyone and everyone contributing anything for the good of the cause. I'm more aware now than ever that the world is not about perfection: it's about progress, ethics, and vision.

- *I dreamed* of developing a platform for others to use as a springboard for achieving their own leadership success, having a balanced life, and serving others.
- *I learned* that it really is better to give than to receive. I learned what it means to be accountable for creating a road map of achievement and how exciting it is to be a positive

factor in someone else's success. Our business and personal missions should strive to lead others, as the people who have touched us with their high standards have led us.

- *I did more* by starting two new companies. One is a nonprofit with a strategic alliance to my consulting/keynote business, the other is with my business partner and friend, Andy Klausner. We established the *Consult P³* (turning potential into profit through people, planning, and processes) and the *Consult P³* University formula for enhancing business systems and personnel in corporate America through the use of top-level consultants and teams.

- *I push my limits* every two years mentally and physically. I have done everything from flying in a Russian MiG jet, to sky-diving, to racing cars, to bungee jumping off Victoria Bridge in Africa. I work just as energetically with homeless people and continually search for one-on-one charitable acts of kindness.

- *And I learned to become more* indebted to the people who have believed in me and challenge me to pay it forward. I've become more alert to the fact that children, as well as adults, watch and learn from my actions. And I learned that being flexible in my need to be right is as important as doing the right thing.

By the way, as for those original childhood lessons that give us those first impressions and lasting reflections . . .

- From my absent father and the kids who tormented me, I learned forgiveness.
- From my grandmother, I learned tolerance.
- From my mom, I learned you are never poor if you have people to love, faith in a higher power, and the ability to make your own choices.

Does that make me a leader? I don't know, but I do know it is true that, while my story is one from rags to riches, the greatest of all wealth is found within my family, faith, and friends. Everyone has the ability to lead someone, even if it is herself.

Don't worry about whether or not you think you're worthy to be a leader. Don't miss the opportunities that come your way to create positive, ethical, productive, and inspirational pathways. Others are sure to follow.

The bottom line is leadership is what happens when you've experienced enough in your own life to make clear and ethical decisions that will inspire others to achieve their own dreams and pay it forward. Leaders have learned to overcome change and conflict with courage, compassion, and confidence. It's a responsibility, an honor, a gift, and a commitment never to be taken lightly.

Anne Newbury
One of the Highest-Paid Direct Sales Directors in the World

Where would the world be without our leaders, both in business and in politics, and in reality in all phases of our lives? It's often been said, "Many are called but few are chosen," and these words certainly apply to the role of the leader.

A good leader must be focused on others to achieve the success of her efforts. When you are called upon to lead, you are involved in the lives of many others and your word must be your bond. People need to know their leader is listening to their needs as well as their dreams. Only then can success come for the whole group.

A good leader must have a *vision* for the success of the group and be able to strategize a course of action, for the whole as well as for each individual, which will bring the vision to fruition. If you work at knowing your people well, you can utilize your talents to bring out the best in each person, which in turn will have a major influence on the whole group.

A good leader is not put off by disappointment; she knows that when working with people disappointments will occur. So she plans for more than the minimum allowed so that her let-downs will be fewer.

I would have to say among the many attributes that are necessary to being a leader, the ones that spring to mind the most would be *focus, patience, credibility,* and *discipline,* and it takes a lifetime to perfect these skills. Of course topping these off would be *good communication*!

Focus simply means to follow one course until you're successful. A good leader is driven to work hard with no eye on the clock. It's often been said that executives never reached the top in an eight-hour day, and I must say this is true. Maintaining perseverance toward a worthy goal will bring the results you want.

Having patience means you can spot flaws in the people you direct, and you care enough to correct them individually in order to bring about changes that will help them improve. Change is a necessity in the lives of those who wish success in any venture, but it is not easy to accept. A good leader can assist individuals, who will benefit long-term, with the acceptance of required change.

Credibility means having good character. It's not uncommon to find people who want to lead but lack the personal attributes of truly great leaders. If there is a breakdown in credibility, or if any member of a team feels that favorites are being played, the results will be devastating and good efforts will be lost.

Discipline is leading by example. Display personal discipline in all areas of your life. The members of your team will admire and learn from you. Discipline is an acquired art and many people spend countless hours trying to do all things for all whose lives they affect, which only results in scattering their shots, thereby getting nowhere.

Good communication is the cornerstone of leadership. It allows you to become the mentor, one of the most rewarding aspects of business. It's been said that a mentor is a 'useful opposite.' When you can establish trust with another and guide that person through years of development, you open an entire world that might have never existed for that person.

For the leader, the climb to the top of the mountain is never over; she is motivated for more, driven for better, and success is a lifetime of many accomplishments. In the end, your greatest accomplishment will have been to teach many others in the process. You can establish a legacy of those who will lead future generations in any and all areas of life.

Sherri's Tips:
Be an Authentic Leader with Integrity

Great leadership is the ability to lead by example, provide inspiration, perform ethically, and possess innate integrity. What we do matters; it sets the example for others. Surely great leaders lead by example! A great leader sets the standard, consistently keeping their actions above reproach. Our everyday actions define us as leaders, as people, and as examples for others to follow.

- **Character:** Great leadership is first and foremost about who we are as people; character is at the core! Character defines our principles and values. Great leadership is about genuine respect for ourselves and for others. We must be fair with everyone, listen with care, and be honest.

• **Integrity:** A vital part of a great leadership is integrity. Without integrity, a person will not qualify as a great leader. Integrity is the commitment to do what is right regardless of the circumstances.

• **Helping Others Succeed:** A great leader knows the importance of sharing their paths to success with others. We see potential in others and want to create opportunities for them to grow and advance, and we seek opportunities to empower them to succeed. People fail to be great leaders primarily due to arrogance and ego.

If you possess the qualities of a great leader, you will be a motivator to others, and you will inspire them. People will want to follow you, work hard, and be on your team. After all, the ultimate goal of a great leader is to motivate and inspire a team toward a common goal.

"Finally, all of you should be of one mind.
Sympathize with each other. Love each other as brothers
and sisters. Be tenderhearted, and keep a humble attitude.
Don't repay evil for evil. Don't retaliate with insults when people
insult you. Instead, pay them back with a blessing.
That is what God has called you to do,
and he will bless you for it."
—I Peter 3:8-9 NLT

14

Self-Care
and
Appreciation

"Every day, in every way, I am getting better and better."
—Emile Coue

There's a reason for the expression "clothes make the woman." Clothing is about confidence; it helps you look the part as well as feel the passion. However, it can be helpful to remember where we came from; most of us weren't born with a designer wardrobe or an Ivy League education, yet we still got where we are today!

Sherri Elliott-Yeary

Most of us have a tendency to take our life for granted on a daily basis. We go about our lives without giving thought to our mortality, taking our health for granted and ignoring the needs of our bodies. But in the moments when we are fully aware, we can't but help feel and appreciate the greatest gift bestowed on us: the gift of being alive. When we live in the moment, we experience just how precious life is, and we care for it as we would a newborn child. If we were always this aware, we would live in awe of the miracle of our existence.

Each day we are faced with a multitude of choices. We decide what we will eat, how much rest and exercise we will give our bodies, and at what pace we will go about our daily activities. It's so easy to forget that our bodies are a delicate gift, a temporary home for our souls. It's usually only in times of great pain, such as when we are faced with the death of a loved one or a serious illness, that we are aware of the importance of life.

Do you ever find yourself trying to live your life like someone else you believe is more acceptable than you? Does your heart cry out for freedom to be accepted for who and what you are right now? I believe that many, if not most, women feel this way at some point in their lives. But it isn't a very enjoyable way to live. Women who don't accept themselves usually have difficulty getting along with others.

I had a hard time with relationships until, through the Word of God, I finally realized that my problems in getting along with others were rooted in my difficulties with myself. I did not like my personality. I constantly compared myself with other women, found fault with myself, rejected myself, and even hated the woman looking back at me in the mirror. God helped me discover that I am not weird; I am unique! And because unique things are rare, they are more valuable.

If you are a rare, one-of-a-kind, valuable, and precious woman, I want to help you learn how to be successful at being yourself! Now I can enjoy the freedom to be myself and I have discovered that self-acceptance and appreciation are two of the greatest gifts.

Now is the time to stop pretending to be someone else and start being who you really are. Remember this: God will never anoint you to be anyone other than your true self. Let now be your time to go forward and be set free from the torments of comparison and trying to be someone you are not. The only thing that stands between you and victory is *you*.

As I've reflected on my journey to achieving my personal and career goals, I have been forced to face certain realities in my life and accept the truth of what I was seeing, hearing, and feeling. I stood back and examined my daily routine and schedule as if it were happening to a good friend, and I asked myself, "What advice would I give this busy lady?" My response was, "Breathe deeply and enjoy the moment so you can be prepared to tackle whatever new challenges are in store for you."

As women, we need to give ourselves loving reminders as we run 150 miles per hour with our hair on fire, trying to live the dream. We need to thrive, not just survive. To have the energy to live life my way, I realized I needed to make a few adjustments. The habits I formed as a child had always worked for me, or so I thought until I looked in the mirror. I had to reclaim my physical energy and lose weight. Thank God for vanity; it really does have an upside.

Physical energy is essential not only for a healthy life but also for *any* success. It requires exercise, sleep, and a health-maintenance plan. But when do we make the time to do that for ourselves? Too many of us wait until something bad happens, like an illness or job loss, before we allow ourselves to put our needs first. These are the questions I asked myself: "Am I really happy?" "Where do I feel truly satisfied?" "What do I want out of life and what changes need to occur to achieve balance?"

A few years ago, I looked into a changing room mirror and saw a future I didn't want suddenly flash before my eyes. I weighed

258 pounds and wore a size twenty-two. I am only five foot two, but up to this point, I had convinced myself that I was simply big-boned. My mom, who is sixty-five years old, is wheelchair-bound as a result of MS, and she has type II diabetes. I was on my way to becoming just like her. That was the moment I understood with clarity the changes I needed to make. A fire ignited in my heart and I sprang into action.

The number one reason for my newfound dedication to living a healthier lifestyle was my daughter, Khirsten. I wanted to be able to play and run with her and my grandchildren someday and knew if I wanted to fully enjoy all of the gifts life had to offer, I had to change—and soon.

As women, we are very aware of our bodies. When we look good, we feel good, and vice versa. I lost more than one hundred pounds because I wanted to be able to fully experience life and not miss out on a moment.

I know having a healthy, energetic body past age forty is a perfectly realistic goal. Looking like a hot twenty-year-old in low riders won't happen, and aiming for that will rob you of the enjoyment of your healthy body.

One of the gifts I received as a result of surviving a personal crisis was the motivation to reevaluate my life and take note of what really matters. Self-care is not a dirty word. Stay healthy. Your life and love will depend on it.

Paulette Martsolf

Designer and Owner of Allie-Coosh

Starting my own high-end clothing boutique, Allie-Coosh, was a dream of mine for many years and has enhanced my life beyond belief. I started this dream twenty years ago, not motivated by money, but by a desire to do what I really love.

I make an effort to eat healthy and fuel my body with the energy it needs for my busy schedule, but I do love to wind my day down with a glass of wine and a soothing bath. As the designer of Allie-Coosh, I have a passion for new and exciting things. I am always dreaming, planning, and creating the next thing. I'm convinced that feeding my soul this way leads to good health, physically and mentally.

As part of my business, image is important to me. When I look as good as I can, I am ready to take on my day. My attitude is positive and upbeat! This is not a trial run; let's enjoy life!

I think women are beautiful and fashionable at every age and size. We each need to find our own sense of style and turn our unique features into assets instead of always criticizing our bodies!

The most important and rewarding part of owning Allie-Coosh has been employing people. I've watched the staff at Allie-Coosh raise their children, send them to college, and embrace their grandkids. Allie-

Coosh could not be what it is today without their help. My days are truly filled with happiness!

Every day is a new beginning. I cannot wait to start the day, and I realize and appreciate the wonderful life I live.

Luane McWhorter

Spa Owner

Many of us have so many responsibilities in life that we forget to take care of ourselves. While it's hard to prioritize something like taking a bath when you have so many other priorities in life, self-care is an important aspect of stress management. Massages, soaks in the tub, or other forms of pampering revitalize you inside and out. And taking time to treat your body like the temple it is has other benefits.

- **Self-Care and Your Physical Health:** While pampering yourself doesn't always lead to major improvements in overall health the way healthy diet and exercise do, the relaxation you get from it can trigger the *relaxation response,* which can prevent *chronic stress* from damaging your health, so, in a sense, self-care is good for your overall well-being.
- **Self-Care and Your Emotional Health:** Taking time out to care for yourself can remind you and others that *your* needs are important too. Having a body that is well cared for can make you feel good about yourself and your life and conveys to others that you value yourself. This can contribute to long-term feelings of well-being.
- **Self-Care Makes You a Better Caretaker:** People who neglect their own needs and forget to nurture themselves are in danger of deeper levels of unhappiness, low self-

esteem, and feelings of resentment. Also, people who spend their time only taking care of others can be at risk of getting burned out on all the giving, which makes it more difficult for them to care for others or themselves. Taking time to care for yourself regularly can make you a better caretaker for others.

Taking a few hours for a spa experience and some much-deserved self-care is also an effective way to manage stress for the following reasons:

- **A Break from Stress:** Taking a break amongst warm bubbles in a tub or under the warm hands of an experienced masseuse can help you feel like you're escaping a stressful reality and taking a mental and emotional vacation. As mentioned, pampering yourself triggers the relaxation response and allows you to come back to the reality of your life feeling refreshed and rejuvenated.

- **Time Alone:** While different people have varying degrees of introversion and extro-version, spending some time alone is important for most people's functioning. When you're relaxing by yourself, it's much easier to slip into a state of quiet meditation, enjoy some self-reflection, or let your problems work them-selves out in the back of your mind without taking all of your focused concentration.

- **Soothing Feelings:** Giving your body some special treatment is a natural way to relieve stress. Other than keeping your skin soft and your body in good repair, spa-related activities like massages and warm baths have been known to soothe, colicky babies like nothing else can. Such activities continue to be effective tools for relaxation as we get older, but we sometimes forget to utilize them.

Going to a day spa is like going on a mini-vacation. It takes you away from the stresses of your daily life, whatever they may be: work, family, relationships, or general overload. We are so bombarded with daily stress from trying to accomplish too much that finding a way to relax has become a necessity. A day spa provides a way to get away without the expense of a vacation. The "spa experience" of pampering treatments in tranquility is about relaxing, quieting, and detoxifying your mind and your body.

Many people have trouble relaxing and sleeping at night. A massage, body treatment, or facial with the human touch—especially with aromatherapy included—balances the energy of the mind and body and brings you to a state of total well-being.

Our society is touch-starved and stressed from lack of human connection. Because we have become so technology focused, we are not connecting in the same way we used to. Having a spa treatment gives the client a human connection in a relaxing and professional environment. Clients are given advice on how to take better care of their skin, hair, and nails as well as how to relax and detoxify.

According to the American Medical Association, 75 percent of disease and illness is stress related; some day spas have evolved into wellness centers and medical spas. A medical spa is a hybrid between a medical clinic and a day spa that operates under the supervision of medical doctor and is sometimes called a "med spa" or a "medi-spa." The spa industry as a whole has reached out to the medical community, knowing that massages and relaxing body treatments go hand in hand with many health issues that result from stress. Having a spa treatment on a regular basis can help keep you calm and centered and keep your muscle fatigue in check. People who take better care of themselves tend to have less stress-related health issues.

In addition to pampering yourself, more substantial forms of self-care involving healthy lifestyle choices are important, too. Eating a *healthy diet*, getting *regular exercise*, and being sure you *get enough sleep* are all important for long-term health and stress management.

Debbie Slade Smith

Corporate Work-Balance Coach

As the saying goes, "nothin' says lovin' like somethin' from the oven." If down-home-southern-fried-buttery-goodness is an expression of love, as a child growing up in Texas with life centered around food, I was adored! I was blessed with grandmothers and a mother who modeled unselfish devotion to family, church, and community; they were known as much for their big hearts as they were for being great Southern cooks.

At age ten, little "Debbie Jean" was the heaviest child in the fifth grade classroom. I had to wear sack dresses, which my precious grandmother handmade, and endure the not-so-nice name calling naïve little boys seem to master at that age.

By high school, my body and my friendships with boys had greatly changed for the better, but as I continued yo-yo dieting for the sake of my looks, I turned to food as comfort and reward even as I was raising my own family. I also was running scared from what I saw in my grandmothers: the legacy of the younger one taking care of the older. All of these women were a mirror images of the others. They were overweight; diabetic, and suffered from memory loss, stroke, and a myriad of other complications. Finally it was my mother's turn. I watched her decline in health as she stretched to take care of family, career, and my grandmothers until each of them passed.

Then my mother died. After courageously battling and winning the war against breast cancer two times, she succumbed to heart disease. It was obvious that mom was a caregiver and took great care of everyone but herself. To her, self-care was selfish; she thought health and wellness were ominous terms simply unattainable by the average woman. That was my wake-up call. I knew I wanted to be here for my precious sons and their children. I began to look at food as fuel for my body and decided to make exercise a priority, not a luxury.

And that is why I "Go Red." *Go Red for Women*™ is the American Heart Association's grassroots effort to let every woman know that heart disease does not have to be our number one killer. Woman to woman, let's share that heart disease is largely preventable. Our biology does not have to be our destiny. Good health and well-being are attainable with small daily steps. This in turn leads to a lifelong journey of mental, physical, and spiritual well-being.

Being chosen to serve on the first national team of women spreading the "Go Red" message has been a way to honor my mom. It changed the direction of my career as it ignited a passion to champion wellness and work–life balance in the corporate marketplace through my own company. As Mother Teresa once said, "We can do no great deeds, only small ones with great love."

I smile now as I remember putting on a pair of red shoes

to celebrate Mom's love of life and my decision to take my life in a new direction. And the job requirement for my company? Wear red.

Sherri's Tips:
Refuel Yourself!

Whether you are nurturing a business, a career, a family, an intimate relationship, or a secret dream, your time and energy are the most valuable commodities you possess. No matter how wisely you spend them, the truth is they are limited in supply and are extremely precious.

Productivity and energy both depend on fuel. Just like our cars, when we aren't fueled and properly maintained, we don't run well. When we don't give ourselves the experiences and care that allow us to be at our best, we simply *aren't* our best. We don't perform at our full potential, we don't have our best gifts to give to others, and we don't feel as good as we could. We don't shine.

We all need quality fuel (and I'm talking about a lot more than food here) to power the full, vibrant, unique life that only we can live. Here are some simple steps to nurturing yourself so you are well primed for the actions you want to take (and whatever else life throws at you).

Check in with yourself. Take a breath, see how your body is feeling, note what's on your mind, and pay attention to your stress level. *Ask yourself what you need.* If it helps, write down the things you need and make sure you get what's on the list, whether it's a water break or stretching your back. Keep the list where you can see it.

Learn to rest when you are tired. When we don't allow ourselves the breaks and rest we need, our ability to focus and concentrate is reduced. Our productivity goes down. We forget things and we stop moving forward. Practice stopping. Rediscover naps. Go to bed on time. If you are getting nowhere on a project, take a five-minute break to do something delightful and refuel your tank.

Do one lovely thing for yourself every day. It's the intention and the follow-through that count here, not the size of the action. It may be giving yourself a pedicure or giving yourself permission to say no to something you don't want to do. It may be flowers on your desk. Give yourself permission for indulgence. Every day.

Start collecting energy boosters. Make a list of small ten-minute acts that make you feel better.

Here are some ideas to get you started:
- Put on music that makes you happy
- Spend a few minutes outdoors
- Change your clothes
- Laugh

- Hug someone you love
- Make a list of your accomplishments
- Stretch, move, or dance around the room

Our flames are our essence. When they are well fed, they hold all of the power of a roaring fire. But our internal flames must be looked after and protected. We must honor them, care for them, tend them, and nourish them. Our job is to protect those flames, knowing that they are our life force and our spirit.

Now I'll give you the sobering news: our choices form our behaviors and our actions. Every choice we make either brings wood to our internal fires or sprinkles a little water on them, diminishing their power. If we wish to stand in all of our light of self-acceptance, live an authentic life, and have the power to bring our purpose to the world, our first commitment must be to keeping our internal fires—our life force—strong. Here are a few examples of choices that can dim your light and some examples of choices that make your flame strong and healthy.

Choices That May Dim Your Light:
- Being around people who criticize you and can't see your magnificence
- "I should"
- "I have to"
- Perceived obligations
- Trying to be nice
- Trying to get other's approval
- Withholding communication
- Lying to yourself
- Gossiping
- Being late
- Not caring about other people's feelings

- Comparing yourself to others
- Judging yourself

Choices That Make Your Fire Roar:
- Having empathy for others
- Taking time for yourself
- Spending time with those you love
- Noticing what you have done well
- Having fun
- Exercising
- Eating a healthy, balanced diet
- Spending your money wisely
- Planning for the future
- Being with people who inspire you
- Appreciating yourself
- Doing charity or volunteer work
- Telling others how much they mean to you
- Going after your dreams
- Forgiving
- Taking responsibility
- Being present and in the moment

My challenge to you: Try out these steps, find what works for you, and add to the list. Then repeat, repeat, repeat. The real key here is getting into the rhythm of paying attention to the amount of fuel you are getting and learning strategies to keep yourself energetic, happy, and thriving.

"So go ahead. Eat your food with joy, and drink
your wine with a happy heart, for God approves of this!"
—*Ecclesiastes 9:7* NLT

15

Unmistakable
Grace

"We make a living by what we get, but
we make a life by what we give."
—Norman Macewan

Sherri Elliott-Yeary

The question that I want this final chapter of the book to address
is not, "Do people really experience moments of grace?" The
question really is, "What do people who experience moments of
grace do afterward?"

Some people who experience grace don't recognize it or
appreciate it. Instead, they brush it aside, write it off, keep quiet
about it, or even try to forget it. Others, like the folks in this
book, share their moments of grace freely, so people everywhere
may be inspired by them and learn from them. I have an idea that
those who do so are helping to heal the world.

So, my friends, it's time to come out of the dark. It's time to wave our hands, to tell our stories, to shout our truth, to reveal our innermost experiences, and let those experiences raise eyebrows and questions that help us turn toward God for answers.

We must share our stories of grace, for it's in these spiritual moments that sacred truths are made real for everyone who hears them. It's how our culture advances and how we evolve; the failure to live those truths causes civilizations to become extinct.

I can think of many avenues God has used to touch my life with His grace; one of them is through my girlfriends. They have loved and supported me through divorce, loss of a job, my daughter's addiction, starting a business, getting married to the man of my dreams, writing my first book, and contributing their personal stories in this, my second book. We only have one life to live, and I feel so fortunate to live life surrounded by women who lift me up.

For me, the definition of grace is the bounty of the relationships I've been blessed with in my life. I have come to believe my life is guided by a powerful and divine force. When I choose to align myself with this force, the best and most advantageous path unfolds before me.

I have also learned there are no coincidences. Every event we experience and every person we meet has intentionally been put in our path to help raise our level of consciousness. When we awaken to this fundamental truth, life becomes a true adventure, a spiritual adventure.

The person who smiles at you while you're walking down the street is no longer a stranger. The phone call from an old friend who crossed your mind the day before is no longer a coincidence. And the failed relationship that left you broken-hearted is no longer a source of bitterness and pain. Instead it's seen as a blessing in disguise, a gift that makes you stronger, more conscious and, ultimately, more alive. Grace shows up in our lives every day; seemingly random events are, in fact, signposts directing us to a new and better life.

I truly believe that, more than anything else, my commitment to live a spiritually based life has been the source of my success. The more I surrender my will to God, the less I've had to worry about how to achieve my goals. Instead, the path finds me. Grace leads me to the exact events and experiences I need at exactly the right time.

I feel the grace of God through the love and support of my family and friends. I thank God for many signs of His grace:

- **My husband, Mason:** He truly accepts me for who I am, warts and all. Mason, I am only a shadow of myself without you. Your direction, support, and encouragement pick me up when I fall; your interest, insight, and suggestions fuel me when I'm drained. You love me deeply, selflessly, and passionately. You complete me. I am blessed to have you as my partner in life. I love you.
- **My daughter, Khirsten:** By living life on your terms, you have shown me what true strength is. I am very proud to be your friend and mom.
- **Jessica and Meredith:** Thank you for the gift of allowing me to be in your lives.
- **My mother:** You gave me the gift of life.
- **My girlfriends:** You love and accept me the way I am. Many of you gave your time and support by contributing to

this book, and your stories have inspired me to be a better person. Your encouragement energized me and motivated me to do something I never thought I could have done—share my most personal self.

- **My adoptive family:** As a troubled twelve-year-old girl, the caring and loving Ford family recognized I was worth something and took me into their home. They showed me what a real family looks like and this became the cornerstone of my new life. Thank you.

- **My family:** You are my reminder of where I come from. We are always going to be connected. I love each of you.

Dr. Mason Yeary

Family Dentist Specializing in Cosmetic Dentistry and Dental Implants

What made Sherri attractive to me was who she is as a person. The real beauty of a person is so much more than physical beauty. When a person walks through my office door, I can tell a lot about that person just by how they treat my staff and by their body language. I became attracted to Sherri's confidence.

When Sherri and I first met, we were both married to other people. She came to me as a new patient and her goal was to have a perfect smile. I was her dentist for five years and gave her the smile she always wanted.

During visits to the office, she would talk with my staff members, all of whom are women. Many times they asked her how she was losing weight. I did not know Sherri ever weighed 258 pounds. To me her weight was never an issue; I just saw an incredible woman who carried herself well.

Since we met, Sherri's physical appearance has changed and she is certainly beautiful, but I was never aware of the changes because what I noticed was her confidence and fiery personality. Those qualities were what won me over.

We talked a lot over the years and became good friends. She really made me think about some things. I liked how I felt when I was around her. I think her clarity and strength make Sherri very attractive and magnetic.

Sherri had gone through a divorce, and I was in the midst of my divorce when she published her first book, *Ties to Tattoos,* and was on the road more than two hundred days a year. Then she became involved in the hiring of 1,900 people for WinStar World Casino and lived on-site in Oklahoma for a long period. If she was ever in town long enough, I was confident I would have the courage to ask her out on a date!

I was searching for what I wanted and trying to decide what I was willing to do to get it. What I decided was that I wanted a real partner as my wife.

Once we had the opportunity to spend time together outside of the doctor–patient relationship, we realized that we had really loved each other for a long time. We did not want to waste another minute. We got married the following January in our living room with no stress or fuss, just us and the intention of spending the rest of lives together.

As a healthcare provider, I'm a pleaser. That's my personality and it makes me a great dentist. I make decisions based on compassion and put myself last instead of first; as one who strives to please others, it was a change for me not to take the path of least resistance.

Sherri demanded my full attention, honesty, and presence. If we were going to be together, she wanted to know that she would not be sitting on the sidelines while I cared for everyone else first. On one of our first dates, she said, "I'm never getting married again or moving again." She had a condo in Frisco, had a great career, and said she "didn't need anything else" unless she was going to be "worshipped, cherished, and adored," as she likes to say. I knew if I was going to win her over and marry her, I needed to do just that. She deserved it.

Sherri stretches me every day to recognize what I really want and to not just do what everyone else wants. When she asks me, "What do you want for dinner?" I can no longer say, "Whatever you want is fine with me." Sherri won't accept that, and she makes me powerfully choose what I want, even when it comes to the little stuff. It's about recognizing what matters to you and making choices you can live with personally.

Sherri was so certain about what she wanted out of a relationship and the rest of her life. At that time, I wasn't as self-aware. Her ability to powerfully choose gave me the clarity to make the best choice for my life. I finally discovered that there is a better way to live than simply taking the path of least resistance, which was how I had lived my life.

Sherri is the first person I have ever met that has this amount of clarity and thought. A lot of us bump through life instead of taking the time to think about our careers, personal lives, or being truly honest with ourselves. What do I want out of this job, this relationship, my life? These are big questions, and it takes time to find the right answers.

We know we are blessed to have this kind of marriage and love for each other, as well as having careers we love and enjoy. These immense blessings rarely come along, so if you have the opportunity, grab them and don't let go.

I am now choosing to fully participate and engage in every decision. The transition wasn't so hard from a choosing-the-restaurant standpoint. The trick is learning to be aware that you have a choice about what you really want and allowing the other person to please you. It's all about participating in a relationship and allowing that other person to get to know your wants.

Sherri and I spend a lot of time talking. That's probably the biggest change for me. We connected at that level first, as friends. She made me share things with her that I didn't talk to anybody about. She was very tuned in to what would allow me to feel good about sharing. I do fall back into old habits sometimes, but she won't let me get away with it for long, and that's what makes our relationship what it is.

I've never met anyone like Sherri. One day, we were getting out of the car and I told her, "You're a handful." She asked, "Is that a good thing?" And I said, "It's just the truth, that's what I love about you.

You're a challenge because you demand what you want, and that makes you a handful." I couldn't have given her a better compliment.

For anyone who wants a great relationship, I would say, "Do it Sherri's way: don't settle for anything less than what you want; the man will either step up to the challenge or shrink away." Either way, you are a winner for not settling for anything less than what you deserve.

Sherri's Tips: Appreciate the Grace in Your Life

If today were your last day on this earth, would you be content with your life so far?

Make a quick list.
1. In column A, list how you would be remembered if today were your last day on earth.
2. In column B, list how you would like to be remembered.
3. In column C, list what steps you need to take to change your life.

When you feel frustrated, take out this list and read it. In my experience, the most exciting and beneficial opportunities have always taken more time than I would have expected or liked. And they have always been worth the wait. As my husband once told me, I am a handful, and patience has never been my strongest characteristic, but I am learning.

Give it all you can. There will be days when you don't feel like giving your best. Give your best anyway for that day. True, it might not be your greatest day, but give all you have every day.

Keep a journal. Write down what you accomplish every day; this will reinforce the progress you are making. Just a few words will do, otherwise you will create yet another job, which you don't need.

Celebrate your achievements! Reward yourself with predetermined gifts. Even a walk in the park would be a worthy reward for a short-term goal! For your ultimate goals, give yourself the greatest reward. Once you have achieved your goals, set new ones. You can always achieve more!

Associate with people like yourself who enjoy the same kinds of pursuits. Offer support to your peers; they will then in turn be there for you when you need them most.

"For the Lord God is our sun and our shield.
He gives us grace and glory. The Lord will withhold no
good thing from those who do what is right."
—*Psalm 84:11* NLT

Helpful Hints on How to Use This Book

I am thrilled that you are passionate about living a life that is intentional and are willing to explore new avenues to have it all. You've made the conscious decision to live your life with uncommon joy—even when the road gets tough!

I lived with frustration and pressure for years until I received a revelation from God about how to get un-frazzled and enjoy the abundant life He had planned for me.

For me, sharing my story and the insights of others with you through this book has been a sign of God's grace. I feel directed by God to help you use this book to enhance your faith and grow as a believer.

When you find yourself questioning the existence of grace, close your eyes, take a deep breath, ask to be taken to the page that will provide you with insight, and open the book to a random page. Trust me—this really works!

Spread the Message to Others

Invite a small group of girlfriends to your home and start your own Passionate Organization of Women (POW) group. Your purpose can be learning to *improve your ability* to see the signs of grace and hope.

- Schedule a monthly meeting and assign a chapter of *You Can Have It All, Just Not All At Once!* to read beforehand. Have each member discuss how she implemented the ending chapter tips and come prepared to share with the group.

- Ask each person to bring her favorite passage or story from the book along with a personal story that relates to the topic.

- Ask each guest or member of your group to bring used clothes and shoes to help support the local domestic violence charity in your neighborhood. You will support others while supporting your own personal growth.

- For further inspiration and support between meetings, take note of how living an uncommon life of joy has touched your life so you can share examples with each other via e-mail or a blog.

- Here are a few questions that can be used for group discussion:
  » How has the power of grace already influenced your life?
  » When did you experience a moment of truth? What happened?
  » What tools have been most helpful to you on your spiritual journey?
  » What evidence of joy and grace have you uncovered from your past?
  » Who are the significant spiritual change agents in your life?

» When were you faced with a situation that forced you to surrender? What happened?

» How has your life changed as a result of using the tips in this book?

» Can each of you share an example of how you've been a conduit of grace and inspiration for others?

To find out more about how to start your own POW
or Wine & Women group, please feel free to contact me at:
sherri@generationalguru.com
or visit my website, www.GenerationalGuru.com,
or my blog, www.RealWomenHavingItAll.com.

Conclusion

You Can Have It All, Just Not All At Once! is a lifelong adventure. In the beginning of this book, I asked what choices you would have to make to live a rich and powerful life in every aspect, from your health to your relationships, career, spiritual walk, and finances. It's my hope and desire that you have discovered some of the answers to those questions within these pages. I also trust that you have renewed your commitment to reach for and grab the life you crave.

You already have everything it takes to live an empowered life; you just need to access it. Each time you stop, slow down, and make the choice to nourish your soul, you will give yourself the confidence to refuel for your journey to the destination of your dreams. If you focus on living a life of uncommon joy and passion, you will have it all!

The tips shared in each chapter have served me, my girlfriends, and my clients for more than a decade as we activated and achieved our climb to success. I know they can serve you equally well. I encourage you to embrace the strength and courage within you—the fire, intuitive vision, engagement, integrity, endurance, enterprise, and renewal—to achieve the passionate life that awaits you. When you summon these strengths, there is no limit to what you can achieve.

The courage to commit to a passionate life is easily within the grasp of every woman. What I know is, when women bond together in pursuit of our individual visions, we are a force of nature that can do extraordinary things.

Ultimately you are the only one who can change the direction of your life. No one can do it for you. People can tell you again and again that you are headed down the wrong path, but until you see it for yourself, until you get tired of going around in circles, nothing will change. No one can choose the destiny of your life; no one can make you take a particular path except you. You get to pick which path you travel: the path to nowhere or the path to the destination of your dreams, your extraordinary life. You choose.

It's been my honor and privilege to share this time together.

Contributors' Index

CHAPTER 1: IF YOU REALLY HAVE IT ALL, YOU PROBABLY WANT TO GIVE SOME BACK!

- **JoAnna Couch**, MS, CPC, is the founder of The Corporate Educator, an executive and employee coaching and training firm. She has been a business professor, seminar leader, teacher, public speaker, national radio show guest, and coach for more than fifteen years. After completing a master's degree in business and psychology, she began consulting and training in major corporations and small businesses. JoAnna works with entrepreneurs, small business owners, employee groups of Fortune 500 companies, schools, and other groups. See: www.CorporateEducator.net.

CHAPTER 2: UNEXPECTED ROADBLOCKS

- **Karla K. Morton**, the 2010 Texas Poet Laureate and a member of the Texas Institute of Letters, has been described as "one of the more adventurous voices in American poetry" and has been featured on *Good Morning Texas*, NPR, *ABC News*, *CBS News*, and in countless newspapers, blogs, and magazines. Her poetry, which spans many subjects and forms, has been published in a variety of literary journals. Karla enjoys promoting poetry and serves as a founding member of the Greater Denton Arts Council and the Denton Poets' Assembly. She is also a member of Western Writers of America and the Writer's League of Texas. See: www.KKMorton.com.

- **Gail Penry** is a native Dallasite with more than three decades of experience as a marketing executive and banker specializing in loans for businesses owned by women. Soon after receiving a devastating diagnosis of lupus, she was forced to leave the workforce when a seizure destroyed her inner ear and balance. After exhausting her lifetime savings and medical insurance, Gail lives on disability and Medicare, but she remains upbeat. On her good days, she volunteers her time and energy supporting her favorite politicians and issues and sends educational e-mails out to the public on behalf of various organizations.

CHAPTER 3: MOMENTS OF CHOICE

- **April Vaughn-Donovan** is the owner of Snelling Staffing Service-North Texas, which serves the communities of Sherman and Denton. A former debutante from Lafayette, Louisiana, April started her company with a family loan and has turned it into a $10 million business. She is a graduate of Millsaps College, is happily married to her soul mate, and has two wonderful children. See: www.Snelling.com.

- **Jan West Tardy** is the founder of Tardy and Associates, a business etiquette and protocol consulting firm. Her mission is to make the world a more civil place one person at a time. Jan graduated from West Texas A&M with a degree in business, and she is certified by The Protocol School of Washington. She is a faculty member of Consult P³, a Dallas-based business systems and personnel enhancement consulting firm. See: www.TardyAndAssociates.com.

- **Kathy Garland,** CMEC, is known as the "Make It Happen Business Coach"; she specializes in helping women achieve greater success. Kathy is a popular speaker and columnist and has spoken to many organizations— including eWomenNetwork, General Electric Women's Network, Texas Business Women, Women of Visionary Influence, Metro Area Professional Saleswomen, National Association of Women Business Owners, Business and Professional Women, WorldWIT International Conference, IABC, and PRSA—on branding and leadership topics. Kathy creates unique experiences for women at all levels to ignite their imaginations to envision a new future. See: www.KathyGarland.com.

CHAPTER 4: FAMILY, FRIENDS, AND RELATIONSHIPS

- **Helene Terry** is an award-winning kitchen and bath designer and the senior design consultant at Bentwood of Dallas. Helene's work has been published in *This Old House*, *Kitchen and Bath Business*, NKBA Profile, *D-Home*, *Texas Home and Living*, and *Great American Kitchens*. She is a board member of the ASID Dallas Design Community, on the Board of Directors for Dallas Executives Association, and on the Kitchen Advisory Committee at The Art Institute of Dallas. See: www.BentwoodOfDallas.com.

- **Kimberly Davis** is the founder of OnStage Leadership, an innovative leadership program that uses tools from the world of theatre to expand effectiveness, build confidence, and set the stage for more powerful connections with employees, customers, and colleagues. With more than twenty years of platform experience, Kimberly offers coaching and leadership programs for individuals and corporations. See: www.OnstageLeadership.com.

- **Dea Richard** has been in the staffing industry for more than twenty years. She has won numerous awards in service, sales, and leadership and is the director of business process integration for US Operations, one of the world's largest staffing organizations. Widowed at age twenty-six and again at age forty-one, Dea is the mother of two teenage boys.

- **Donna Bender** is the founder of The Donna Bender Company, a branded marketing and promotional strategies company with a specialty in assisting corporations, small businesses, and entrepreneurs to build and reinforce their brand through customized marketing, promotions, and advertising choices. Donna's twenty-five-year career in marketing and advertising has included working as a vice president at Calvin Klein, running the women's division of Salvatore Ferragamo, and devoting her talent and experience as a marketing consultant. She serves on the Professional Advisory Council for The School of Fashion & Retail Management at the Art Institute of Dallas, is a board member of The Fashion Group International, and owns a certified woman-owned business. See: www.DonnaCo.com.

CHAPTER 5: MEN, WOMEN, AND THE WORKPLACE

- **Judy Hoberman** is a speaker, sales trainer, educator, and coach specializing in gender communications. She is the author of *Selling In A Skirt*, a book that offers unique insights into the challenges and opportunities sales professionals face when communicating with the opposite gender, whether a coworker or a client. She is considered one of the foremost gender and sales specialists in the country. See: www.SellingInASkirt.com.

- **Jackie Agers,** MEd, LPC, is a family therapist specializing in emotional, behavioral, and communication-based issues, including therapy for depression, grief counseling, parenting support, couples counseling, work and career counseling, cultural, gender and identity problems, and other family and work-related therapies. See www.JackieAgers.com.

- **Dr. Sue Hummel** is an associate professor at the Baylor College of Dentistry and is the director of removable prosthodontics. She and her husband, Dr. Larry Pace, have a dental practice in Dallas. Susan and Larry are empty nesters who spend their spare time hunting, working with their Brittany Spaniels, traveling, and visiting family. Susan plays the violin and does exquisite hand quilting and sewing. See: www.TAMBCD.edu.

CHAPTER 6: MONEY, MONEY, MONEY

- **Jean Danner** is the director of employee relations for Tenet Healthcare Corporation, a company with fifty-seven thousand employees. Her specialties include the delivery and execution of high-quality HR programs and services. She holds an MBA in human resources from the University of Dallas, a BS in human development and psychology, a BS in business administration and personnel management from the University of Wisconsin, Green Bay, and has earned the SPHR professional designation. See: www.TenetHealth.com.

- **Lisanne Glew** is a financial advisor with a US investment firm in Dallas, Texas. She is an accredited wealth management advisor (AWMA) with twenty-five years in the financial services industry. Lisanne focuses on executive compensation, wealth management services, and executive client relationship management. She is a board director for The Board Connection, a nonprofit dedicated to increasing the number of women on corporate boards and an active member of Girl Scouts of North East Texas' Alumnae Association. Lisanne holds a degree in law and an MBA from the University of Toronto, Canada.

Chapter 7: The Power of Yes and No

- **Dr. Eileen Dowse**, founder of Human Dynamics, is an innovative, results-oriented human resources leader with extensive experience in organizational development, executive coaching, human relations, and facilitation. Human Dynamics provides coaching and counseling to executives and leaders from a variety of industries in the areas of performance, productivity, career transition, and workplace dynamics. Industries served include high technology, manufacturing, government, research and development, and higher education. See: www.Human-Dynamics.com.

- **Karen Hunt** brings more than twenty-five years of sales, marketing, and business development experience to the addiction field. She is known for her creative and strategic marketing abilities. For the last six years, her outstanding top performance has been noted at three top treatment organizations, and she has established herself in the industry for building strong core relationships and exceptional customer service. Karen received her graduate marketing certificate from Southern Methodist University's Cox School of Business. She is a member of the Dallas Chamber of Commerce, American Marketing Association, Nexus Auxiliary, Dallas and Fort Worth Medical Societies, and Eating Disorder Hope.

- **Tere Bettis** is a human resources business partner supporting the Corporate Finance Group with Anadarko Petroleum in Houston, Texas. Her specialties are training, interviewing, and recruiting. She attended Oklahoma City University. She and her husband, Lonny, have been married for thirty-eight years and have a daughter.

CHAPTER 8: LIVE AN EMPOWERED LIFE AND FOLLOW YOUR PASSION

- **Maura Schreier-Fleming** is a results-oriented speaker, trainer, and consultant who has worked with numerous clients to improve sales performance. Maura works with business and sales professionals who want to get better results from their work. She is the founder of Best@ Selling, a consultancy focused on real-world selling skills and strategy. She is a guest columnist and popular media personality, and she serves on the faculty of Consult P³. See: www.BestAtSelling.com.

- **Anne Spoon** is the artist behind Anne Spoon Fine Art. She is a graduate of the School of Visual Arts in Manhattan and moved to Oklahoma from upstate New York in 1991 to be with her husband and to pursue a full-time career as an artist. She has studied with C. W. Mundy, Dan Gerhartz, Matt Smith, and Sherry McGraw. She never stops learning and perfecting her light- and color-filled paintings of people, places, and things. Her work has been featured in numerous shows, including the Greenhouse Gallery Salon International and the American Women Artists Biannual Show, and she is a recipient of the Shirl Smithson Memorial Scholarship given by the Oil Painters of America. See: www.AnneSpoon.com.

- **Eve Mayer Orsburn** is the CEO of Social Media Delivered, one of the largest social media optimization companies serving clients worldwide with consulting, training, and managing social media services. Ranked by *Fast Company* magazine as one of the 100 Most Influential People Online, Eve speaks professionally to groups on the Social Media Equation, which is her proven system for how organizations must engage in media to generate a positive ROI. She maintains an online network of more than eighty thousand fans, followers, and connections every day. Eve is the author of *Social Media for the CEO: The Why & ROI of Social Media for the CEO of Today and Tomorrow.* See: www.SocialMediaDelivered.com.

CHAPTER 9: RECOGNIZING OPPORTUNITIES

- **Shelly Little** is the CEO of Michaels Wilder. Shelly has more than twenty years of experience and multiple areas of expertise. Her wide range of professional pursuits, from HR generalist work to independent consulting, help her approach client problems with creativity and innovation. With a specialty in developing recruiting solutions for her clients, Shelly is equally as skilled in diagnosing her clients' business challenges in areas like benefits, training, or performance appraisals. See: www.MichaelsWilder.com.

- **Kathy Light** is the founder and president of Kathy Light International, a company dedicated to inspiring leaders to realize their greatness and achieve their visions. She provides action-oriented coaching, facilitation, training, speaking, and consulting. Kathy completed her undergraduate degree in fine arts at Texas Christian University and earned an MBA from the University of St. Thomas in Minneapolis, Minnesota. She is a member of the International Coach Federation (a globally recognized association of professional personal and business coaches) and the National Speakers Association, and is certified to administer a number of professional development assessments. See: www.KathyLight.com.

CHAPTER 10: BETTER OR BITTER—THE CHOICE IS YOURS!

- **Niesha Alexander** is a single mother of four boys, is extremely driven and motivated, and 2011 ventured out to start her own business as a virtual assistant. Niesha offers administrative support to small business owners. Combining her twelve years of administrative skills and project management experience, Niesha offers her clients a wide range of support. Niesha was born in Los Angeles, California, and now resides in Plano, Texas, with her four boys. See: www.YourVirtualProjects.com.

CHAPTER 11: OVERCOMING ADVERSITY

- **Mary Golaboff,** SPHR, is a human resources consultant who specializes in compliance, audits, policies and procedures, employee relations, leadership development and training, and health and wellness initiatives. She is a faculty member of Consult P³. Mary is a certified Myers-Briggs practitioner. She is a nationally certified senior professional in human resources through the Society of Human Resources Management. Mary graduated from Texas A&M with a BA in business-entrepreneurial. She is a member of SHRM and IREM. See: www.ConsultP3.com.

- **Dr. Venus Opal Reese** is the founder and CEO of Defy Impossible, Inc., a personal and professional development company. Dr. Venus shares her story as an inspirational speaker, motivator, professor, executive mentor, corporate trainer, author, theater artist, and producer of her own brand, Street Smarts: Surviving Threat & Creating New Realities. At age sixteen, Dr. Venus lived on the streets of Baltimore amid violence, drugs, and prostitution. Fourteen years later, she had earned multiple degrees: a BFA from Adelphi University; an MFA in acting and movement theatre from Ohio State University; and an MA in drama and a PhD in performance theory and literary criticism from Stanford University. See: www.DrVenusOpalReese.com and www.DefyImpossible.com.

- **Cindy Colangelo** is the director of CLC Consulting, a consulting firm dedicated to building strategic partnerships between mission-driven nonprofit agencies and the communities they serve. Cindy developed CLC Consulting after a long tenure of working in both the corporate sector as well as nonprofit. She is a graduate of the University of Florida and earned her certificate of non-profit management through Brookhaven College and the Center of Nonprofit Management. See: www.CLCConsulting.net.

CHAPTER 12: YOU ARE WHO YOU ARE SUPPOSED TO BE
- **Blanche Evans** is the cofounder and CEO of EvansEmedia, a copywriting and graphics firm specializing in e-magazines, e-brochures, and e-books. She is an award-winning journalist, the author of five books and more than four thousand columns, and she was featured in Donald

Trump's book *The Best Real Estate Advice I Ever Received*. She is also an award-winning painter and her work is carried at the Mary Tomas Studio Gallery in Dallas. Blanche served as the initial editor for *You Can Have It All, Just Not All At Once!* See: www.EvansEmedia.com.

- **Sarah Spence** is a senior HR generalist employed by one of the largest, most respected cosmetic firms in the world. She provides generalist support to the finance, legal, and IST teams. Sarah has her designation as a professional human resources (PHR) and practices on-going continuing education to stay current on all HR-related topics and best practices. She graduated from Texas Tech University with a bachelor of science degree.

- **Michele Benjamin** is the Midwest regional sales manager for Silkroad Technology. She and her husband, Terry, adopted Nicole, Michele's niece, and are raising her as their own daughter. They are part of a volunteer search and rescue team and own trained rescue dogs that perform searches for missing persons and cadavers.

CHAPTER 13: AUTHENTIC LEADERSHIP
- **Petey Parker** is the CEO of Petey Parker Enterprises, a group of specialty consulting firms devoted to improving the performance of people and processes at every level. Her clients include associations, financial institutions, governments, and nonprofits. Some of her specific clients are Wal-Mart, McGraw-Hill, KPMG, Century 21 National, Southwest Airlines, and the National Association of Realtors. Petey and her business partner, Andrew Klausner, are pioneering the concept of consulting faculty, where busi-

nesses can go to one consultation source for all their needs. The Consult P3 University is one of the only consulting faculties of its kind; it allows companies access to top consultants in many fields, including crisis management, marketing and communications, protocol, human resources, and much more. See: www.PeteyParkerEnterprises.com.

- **Anne Newbury** is a Mary Kay independent elite executive national sales director emeritus. She was honored at the 2006 Mary Kay annual convention as the first Mary Kay independent national sales director to earn more than $1 million in commissions in a single year. During the course of her thirty-seven-year career, Anne earned nearly $11 million, overseeing approximately thirty thousand Mary Kay representatives in eight countries. When Mary Kay passed away in 2001, Anne was asked to serve as the company's media spokesperson, and she appeared on numerous television shows and in newspapers to talk about Mary Kay's life and legacy.

CHAPTER 14: SELF-CARE AND APPRECIATION

- **Paulette Martsolf is** the founder of Allie-Coosh Boutique and the designer of the store's signature clothes. She studied in Toronto and Paris and honed her skills in the industry before launching her own line. She travels to New York, Los Angeles, Paris, and anywhere else fashion trends are made to explore fabrics and accessories and to obtain design inspiration. Each collection is created in her Dallas workshop with styles to flatter every body type. See: www.Allie-Coosh.com.

- **Luane McWhorter** is the owner of the Grand Spa in Dallas and the Sutera Spa in Flower Mound. She is a firm believer in the power of massage and spa treatments as integral components of physical, mental, and spiritual health. See: www.GrandSpa.com and www.SuteraSpa.com.

- **Debbie Slade Smith** is an executive recruiter and fifth-generation Texan. In addition to being a wife and a mother, Debbie is the president of Work-Life Balance Plans, LLC, a corporate vacation benefits specialty site. Debbie is a national spokesperson for the American Heart Association's Go Red For Women campaign and a supporter of The Bridge Breast Network.

CHAPTER 15: UNMISTAKABLE GRACE

- **Dr. Mason Yeary** began his family and cosmetic and family dental practice, Plano Smiles, in 1991. Dr. Yeary has trained with some of the world's most prominent dental specialists and designed his unique practice to offer cutting-edge technology and sedation techniques in a warm and friendly office environment. He and his wife, Sherri, share a passion for charitable work, including providing dental services to abused and battered women through the Attitudes & Attire's Hopeful Smiles program. See: www.PlanoSmiles.com.

Resource Index

The Greenhouse Treatment Facility
The Greenhouse's mission is to provide an enlightened, caring treatment community in which all those affected by drug or alcohol addiction may begin a new life.
Contact: 855-293-7847
www.TheGreenHouse.com

HopeWorks Truth & Wisdom for Life
HopeWorks blends psychological principles with the wisdom of biblical truth to provide help through counseling. HopeWorks is committed to:
- helping each person embrace his or her own self-worth and dignity,
- applying biblical truths and principles as the cornerstone for care,
- providing a complete integration of psychological principles, and
- encouraging clients to make life-affirming choices in order to renew their peace, joy, and hope.
Contact: 972-596-5400
www.HopeWorksCounseling.org

Go Red For Women
Go Red For Women celebrates the energy, passion, and power we have as women to band together to wipe out heart disease and stroke.

In 2004 the American Heart Association (AHA) faced a challenge. Cardiovascular disease had been claiming the lives of nearly five hundred thousand American women each year, yet women were not paying attention. Many even dismissed it as an "older man's disease." To dispel the myths and raise awareness of heart disease as the number one killer of women, the AHA created Go Red For Women, a passionate social initiative, to empower women to take charge of their heart health.

Contact: 1-888-MY-HEART
www.GoredForWomen.org

Overeaters Anonymous

Overeaters Anonymous (OA) offers a program for recovery from compulsive eating using the Twelve Steps and Twelve Traditions of OA. Worldwide meetings and other tools provide a fellowship of experience, strength, and hope where members respect one another's anonymity. OA charges no dues or fees; it is self-supporting through member contributions.

OA is not just about weight loss, weight gain, maintenance, obesity, or diets. It addresses physical, emotional, and spiritual well-being. It is not a religious organization and does not promote any particular diet.

OA members differ in many ways, but they are united by a common disease and the solution they have found in the OA program. They practice unity with diversity and welcome everyone who wants to stop eating compulsively.

Contact: 505-891-2664
www.OA.org

National Domestic Violence Hotline

The National Domestic Violence Hotline was established in 1996 as a component of the Violence Against Women Act (VAWA) passed by Congress. The Hotline is a nonprofit organization that provides crisis intervention, information, and referral to victims of domestic violence, perpetrators, friends, and families. The Hotline answers a variety of calls and is a resource for domestic violence advocates, government officials, law enforcement agencies, and the general public.

The Hotline serves as the only domestic violence hotline in the nation with access to more than four thousand shelters and domestic violence programs across the United States, Puerto Rico, Guam, and the US Virgin Islands. Advocates receive approximately 23,500 calls each month. The Hotline is toll-free, confidential, and anonymous. It operates twenty-four hours a day, 365 days a year, in more than 170 languages through interpreter services, with a TTY line available for the deaf, deaf-blind, and hard of hearing. The staff at The Hotline is also available to provide assistance and guidance in a variety of areas including media, public relations, fundraising, public policy, legal advocacy, and public education and training.

Contact: 1-800-599-SAFE
www.TheHotline.org

The Family Place

The Family Place is the largest family violence service provider in the Dallas area; it reaches out to thousands of victims of family violence each year with award-winning programs that keep women and children safe. For thirty-three years, The Family Place's mission to end the epidemic of family violence has remained constant. They believe that intervention, emergency shelter, and crisis counseling for all victims—women, children, and men—will save lives and that transitional housing and case management will transform lives for the better.

Contact: 214-941-1991
www.FamilyPlace.org

RAINN

The Rape, Abuse & Incest National Network is the nation's largest anti-sexual-violence organization. RAINN operates the National Sexual Assault Hotline and the National Sexual Assault Online Hotline; publicizes the hotline's free confidential services; educates the public about sexual violence; and leads national efforts to prevent sexual violence, improve services to victims, and ensure that rapists are brought to justice.

The RAINN hotlines consist of a nationwide partnership of more than 1,100 local rape treatment hotlines providing victims of sexual violence with free, confidential services around the clock.

Contact: 1-800-656-HOPE
www.RAINN.org

Bridge Breast Network

The concept for the Bridge Breast Network was born in 1992 and was nurtured by a group of breast cancer survivors who met in the office of Sally Knox, MD, a breast specialist at Baylor University Medical Center in Dallas, Texas. Dr. Knox often donated her services to patients in her practice who lacked the resources and insurance coverage for breast cancer treatment. Other physicians were always interested and ready to assist by evaluating and even doing procedures.

The Bridge Breast Network saves lives by linking low income, uninsured individuals to diagnostic and treatment services for breast cancer.

Contact: 1-877-258-1396 (toll-free)
www.BridgeBreast.org

About the Author

Best-selling author Sherri Elliott-Yeary is an internationally recognized expert in the field of generational differences and personal transformation. Sherri's previous book, *Ties to Tattoos: Turning Generational Differences into a Competitive Advantage,* earned her the title of the Generational Guru.

Sherri was raised by a single mother in Canada, and she overcame poverty to become an internationally recognized speaker, author, and coach. She holds university degrees in human resource management, and accounting and risk management, as well as a designation as a senior professional human resources professional (SPHR). She is a lifelong believer in self-improvement and continuing education.

Sherri is CEO of the human resource consulting firm Optimance Workforce Strategies, where she shares her innovative success strategies and expertise in generational differences and other workforce issues. Sherri educates employers on how to bridge generational and gender gaps to help managers and employees work more harmoniously and productively together to achieve a competitive advantage in the marketplace.

Sherri's journey to success began at age twelve, when she was adopted by the Ford family; they made her feel loved and worthy. She discovered that she had the internal fire and desire to achieve uncommon success in her life. She shares that fire and desire with others as a teacher, mentor, and coach, helping women and executives learn how to achieve the life they desire.

Sherri is committed to being known as a woman of God who walks the walk that Jesus has laid out for every one of us. Her mission is to "move, touch, and inspire others to lead a fully authentic life." In addition to lecturing at conferences and to groups across the United States and Canada, Sherri personally leads "You Can Have It All" retreats and workshops, which are profound, two-day, life-changing experiences that inspire self-love and emotional freedom.

Her website, www.GenerationalGuru.com, and blog, www.RealWomenHavingItAll.com, attract thousands of visitors each month who are committed to producing extraordinary results through her numerous teleconferences, community calls, newsletters, and videos.

Sherri and her husband, Dr. Mason Yeary, are the parents of three Millennial-aged daughters. Khirsten resides in Canada; Meredith resides in Plano, Texas; and Jessica and her husband, Stephen, reside in Dallas, Texas. Sherri and Mason make their home in Plano with Coco, their chocolate Havanese.